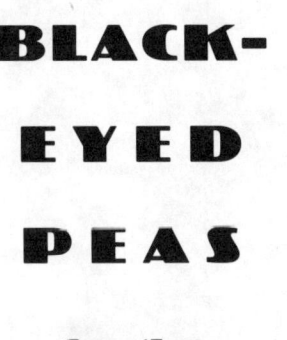

BLACK-EYED PEAS

for the

SOUL

Tales to Strengthen the
African American Spirit and
Encourage the Heart

written and compiled by
Donna Marie Williams

A Fireside Book Published by Simon & Schuster

FIRESIDE
Rockefeller Center
1230 Avenue of the Americas
New York, NY 10020

FIRESIDE and colophon are registered trademarks
of Simon & Schuster Inc.

Designed by Bonnie Leon-Berman
Manufactured in the United States of America

ISBN 1-56865-919-9

To George Walter Williams
and great cooks of the soul everywhere

Contents

Step 3: Soaking the Peas

Our cook learns patience as the peas soak in water. 119

Step 4: Cooking the Peas

Step 5: Eating the Peas

Acknowledgments

Story collecting is a massive undertaking, especially when you don't have much time. Thanks to my excellent writing team for their help, expertise, and support: Laura Williams, Janice Williams, and Gettye Israel.

Thanks to my agent, Denise Stinson, and my editor, Dawn Daniels, for their crucial roles in this project.

The following contributors made this book possible. Many many thanks to all:

Edward Allen, Jr.
Maya Angelou
Atara
Moni Azibo
Bandele Publications
Ruth Beckford
Bertice Berry
Ari Brown
Yvonne Butchee
Mary T. Carr
Shirley Chisholm
Jacqueline Joyner Cissell
Chavunduka and Steve Cobb
Communicators Press
Sarah Delany
Michelle R. Dunlap
Marian Wright Edelman
Gail Erskine
Y. A. Folayan
Stephanie J. Gates

Janice C. Hodge
Karen M. Hurley
Gettye Israel
Jauqo Kelly
James L. Lasenby
Harry Lennix
JoAnn Long
Kecia Lynn
Haki Madhubuti
Estella Conwill Majozo
P. K. McCary
Dwight Anthony McKee
Beverly Phillips McLeod
Ron Mitchell
Ben Mtundu
Nichelle Nichols
E. D. Nixon
Ken Norton
Rosa Parks
Geoffrey R. Pete

Acknowledgments

Wintley Phipps
Alfred "Coach" Powell
Darline R. Quinn
Jocelyn Rials
Ralph Cheo Thurmon
Dawn Turner Trice
John Turk
Morrie Turner

Nora Young Turner
Debora Tutterrow
Iyanla Vanzant
Gloria Wade-Gayles
Rita Coburn Whack
Hyacinth A. Williams
James Williams
Andrew Young

The following individuals gave graciously of their time and life experiences: Thomas L. Berkeley, Dr. Thomas Whittaker Browne, Dr. Ruth Love, Dorothy Smith Patterson, Gay Plair Cobb, and Brenda Payton.

Libations to the following ancestors whose words of wisdom have been captured within the covers of this book:

George Washington Carver
Bessie Delany
Frederick Douglass
Honorable Elijah Muhammad

My family and friends were a constant source of emotional support. My love and gratitude to Lynne and Jeffery Speller, Denise Wimberly, George and Hyacinth Williams, and my wonderful children, Michael and Ayanna.

All praises to God (Him/Her), Jeshua, the angels, the Orisas, the ancestors, and the divine energy that flows through and connects us all.

Introduction

When I got the call from my agent, Denise Stinson, that Dawn Daniels, my editor at Simon & Schuster, wanted me to compile a collection of inspirational African American stories, I was thrilled. "The title will be *Black-Eyed Peas for the Soul*," said Denise. Soul food as a metaphor for inspiration. I liked it, very nice. This was to be the Black version of the enormously successful *Chicken Soup for the Soul*. Then my heart sank.

"Uh, can we change the title?" I asked.

"Why?" asked Denise in her typically blunt manner. I could just see her looking at her watch.

"Because it sounds like a rip-off of *Chicken Soup for the Soul*," I said. I knew that my Africentric friends would give me hell for that title.

"So?"

I sighed. "I'll work on the outline," I said. And I'll come up with another title, I vowed under my breath.

When my concept for the book was okayed, I hit the streets running. I enlisted the services of my sisters, Laura and Janice Williams, and my sisterfriend, Gettye Israel. We begged stories from people we knew to be upbeat and positive and from others who were referred to us. In the

17

process, we got a wide range of reactions to the title, from laughter to "oh Gods" to heads shaking and eyes rolling. But in every case they got it, whether or not they had heard of *Chicken Soup for the Soul*. They knew right away that these were to be stories describing *our* experiences from *our* perspective.

As the stories began to pour in—stories about beginnings, wisdom, patience and endurance, excellence, joy, and miracles—I began to see the wisdom in Dawn's original title.

Black-eyed peas are not a comfort food like chicken soup. When you need a warm shawl wrapped around your body, chicken soup keeps good company, but when you're really in a bind, when there's no one to turn to or there's nowhere left to go, you need the grit, determination, and wisdom of the lowly black-eyed pea to get you through the tough times. Our ancestors sowed them as slaves, and now we can reap their bounty as free, self-determining men and women. Those black eyes have seen us through the bad times and, bless those good luck bowls of Hoppin' Johns, they'll see us to the good. Black-eyed peas, as it turns out, are an excellent metaphor for the sojourn of Africans in America.

Thus, *Black-Eyed Peas for the Soul* is not your ordinary collection of inspirational stories. These stories are grounded in reality, and while many are gritty and disturbing, they all inspire us to shed the shackles of mediocrity and apathy. They challenge us to become better people, more loving, smarter, and more determined than ever before. They teach us never to accept the status quo, always to rebel against evil, and to be radical for righteous causes. They admonish us to take better care of ourselves, to reclaim our children, and take back our communities. Even the last section, with its dreams, prayers, and miracle stories, gives us a vision of the very real spiritual technologies that delivered our ancestors through multiple invasions of our Homeland, the horrors of American slavery, Reconstruction, Jim Crow, injustice, discrimination, and, as Rosa Parks might say, feeling mighty tired of all the mess.

One of the challenges in compiling this collection was getting folks to understand my one irrevocable law. *No witnessing allowed.* Like Martin, I too have a dream, that Black people from all spiritual and philosophical walks of life will begin to speak a common language, unify around issues, become a community again. We can't do this if we continue to allow, as my friend Carolyn Dennis used to say, a pork chop to divide us. We are many in one. We are varieties of Christian, Muslim, New Thought, Buddhist, Yoruba, Agnostic, Hebrew Israelite, Republican, Democrat, Vegetarian, Meat Eating, African-centered, Integrationist, and Universalist.

I had to weed out stories about religious conversions, coming-out-of-the-closet stories, and even one about a man's love for his particular fraternity. What did Mama used to say? If I gave in to one, I'd have to give in to everybody, so I had to be ruthless. Fortunately, I didn't lose any friends over this, as many of the writers who contributed to this collection I've either worked with in the past or knew of my reputation with the red pen.

Although I didn't want to alienate anyone with these stories and the way they were assembled, I knew I might lose a few readers. Some of us may have a real problem with a book that has the audacity to feature a story about astrology along with one that explores the Christian ritual of anointing with oil. And if they loved that combination, they'll really love how the first section includes creation stories from the Honorable Elijah Muhammad and Yoruba priest Ralph Cheo Thurmon, as well as P. K. McCary's hip version of Genesis. Believe it or not, the no-witnessing rule holds fast even with these stories. They do not advocate following a particular path to God; they are telling, from their own unique points of view, stories of how the world was created.

Hairs were split, however, for while no witnessing was allowed, testimonies were. In talking about a particular trial or tribulation, many writers had to talk about the spiritual beliefs that helped them to overcome. That was perfectly acceptable and most appropriate. I started slashing and burning, however, when the writing strayed from sharing to promotion.

Introduction

Black-Eyed Peas taps the rich vein of life experiences that testify to how wonderful and resilient we are as a race of people. The reason why Aesop's fables have endured is because they teach, they socialize, they entertain. Likewise, these black-eyed peas stories feed the soul with insights that are relevant to a twenty-first century people.

Yes, we must know our history, but to tell the truth, if I watch Oprah it's because I want to know what's going on with people *today*. I want to know how people are getting over. Too many of our written stories sing sad songs about strange fruit. We have been in mourning for too long. Never forget, and let's move on to a new millennium, a new dispensation, a promised land that we ourselves can create and enter into. Heaven on earth is about the Divine Connection, self-love, excellence, and a good, hearty bowl of black-eyed peas to get us over the rough spots. As it is said in Yoruba, *agba ibi ire* (may it go to the right spot).

STEP ONE

Buying the Peas

Daddy's kitchen is a modest space. Few of the amenities of a really well-stocked kitchen live here. This kitchen has only the essentials for cooking: a stove, a refrigerator, some pots and pans, a spatula. The kitchen is a lot like my father. He is a man of few needs and possessions. I bought the blender a couple of years ago, and my mother insisted on a microwave oven, but neither feels right in his kitchen. It's like High Tech meets Jurassic Park. My father tolerates their presence, but never uses them.

In the kitchen closet are all the canned goods and other sundries. There are also cookbooks by the dozens, Christmas presents for the man who has everything but never needs anything—especially cookbooks. If he uses a cookbook at all, it's the old reliable Fannie Farmer. The pages are stained with the grease of dishes past. Some are torn. Favorite recipe pages are dog-eared, and a rubber band holds it all together.

Daddy's kitchen serves as both the cooking center and the "formal" dining area, so the kitchen's most always a mess. My mother fusses about it, but it's Daddy's kitchen, and since she wouldn't want to risk pissing him off into retiring from cooking forever, she keeps the fussing to a dull roar.

My father is one of those rare and wonderful men who not only loves to cook, and all the time, but creates the most delectable dishes in all of Creation. Not only that, he has never minded my sisters and me crowding him in his domain, never shooed us away. Over the years, his kitchen became the main place in the house for sharing and talking smack. With a glass of beer in one hand and a stirring spoon in the other, some jazz or blues playing on the old radio, Daddy would listen to hours and hours of his girls talking about men or jobs or children or whatever. He'd just sit there and listen, grooving to the music and the smells of his famous chili, barbecued chicken, garden-grown collards, macaroni and cheese. Intoxicating, hypnotic smells.

Except for one Saturday a few weeks ago. A strange and alien scent entered into Daddy's kitchen, and it was my fault. I brought the kids to visit their grandparents. Truth be told, I needed baby-sitting help. I was on deadline to finish a manuscript and the little darlings were driving me crazy.

I settled at the kitchen table, papers spread all around me, when, just as I was putting pen to paper, my daughter, Ayanna, walked up to me and said, "I'm hungry."

I hate those words "I'm hungry." When I'm hungry, I can just make a sandwich and be satisfied. But when a child is hungry, a good mother has to think about all the major food groups, and today, like most days, I just didn't have the time.

No, tell the truth, Daddy may be the chef of life, but I, his beloved daughter, can't cook worth a jambalaya damn. I wish I could take out a bag of beans and rice and magically produce a five-course meal, but I never got the hang of it. Ashamed, I threw some turkey hot dogs in a pot of boiling water (that much I can do). The scent of boiling meat wafted through the house and, like the cartoons, led my father by the nose to the kitchen.

"You fixing my granddaughter hot dogs?" Daddy said. It was an accusation, which immediately put me on the defensive.

"This is just to hold her." He looked at me suspiciously. "Until I get home and cook her a proper meal."

Daddy didn't buy that lie for one minute. "What you gonna fix her when you get home?" I blinked. "Girl, you know you should be ashamed." I cowered.

"I was going to do quiche. Yeah, quiche."

"Quiche!" He was disgusted. Most days, my father is easygoing, the strong, silent type, but the two things that could send him over the edge were restaurant food and food that didn't make sense. Egg pie didn't make sense to him.

"Mommy, I'm hungry!" Ayanna cried, playing the emerging kitchen drama for all it was worth. Casting me a sideways sneer, my father knelt before my four-year-old on one arthritic knee.

"You want some real food, princess? I got some leftover macaroni and cheese and string beans and chicken. You want that?" he asked, standing up, knees cracking and groaning under the strain. He went to the refrigerator and took out a few foil packages.

"I'm hungry too, Mommy." Michael, my ten-year-old, was always hungry.

"There's plenty enough for both of you. Gone and watch *Rug Rats*. I'll let you know when dinner's ready." My children skipped happily to the TV. Daddy started banging pots and lighting fires. At that moment I couldn't even deal with the issue of too much TV watching and my thus far unsuccessful attempts to eliminate chicken from our diet.

"Daddy, I know how to cook. For real. It's just that I've been so busy trying to make this deadline—."

"Donna, I've always told you, keep a pot of chili or soup on hand. When was the last time you cooked my grandchildren a decent meal?" I blinked. He held up his hand. "Never mind."

"I'm a single parent," I whined. "I've got no help. I've got to do everything myself. Time—" I faltered.

"Thirty-odd years old—how old are you?—and still can't make a decent pot of peas. Hot dogs!"

"I can cook," I said with no conviction. "I do quiche and other dishes the children love. Really."

"Got all them degrees, but you can't cook a decent pot of peas." Then my father looked to the ceiling and asked God, "Where did I go wrong?"

"Brother," I muttered, but I knew I had been caught. I'd been wanting to be a better cook, a better mother, but I had never found the time to fig-ure my way around all the herbs and spices.

"Be here tomorrow, seven o'clock sharp," Daddy said suddenly. "I'ma teach you how to make a decent pot of black-eyed peas."

I looked up at that old man like he had lost his mind. Seven o'clock on a Sunday morning? My one and only day of the week to sleep in late?

"Okay," I sighed.

Fearing my father's wrath and razor tongue, I was at my parents' home, sleep still in my eyes, at 6:59 A.M. My children were excited, though. This felt like an adventure to them—getting up early on a Sunday morn-ing, dressing up for church. Little did they know what they were in for. My mother had agreed to take them to Morning Glory Baptist Church, and they'd probably be there for most of the day. That left me alone to face the Tyrant of the Kitchen.

When the door closed after Grandma and the children, my father and I eyed each other warily. "So what torture do you have in store for me to-day?" I asked brightly. He grumbled, then abruptly told me to "c'mon."

"Where are we going?" I asked, following his limping form out of the house and to his raggedy car, make and model unknown. He didn't an-swer me. "Do we have to ride in that thing?" Still no answer. "Come on, Daddy, let's take my car. See how nice and shiny it is?" He barely glanced my way. Just opened my door, waited for me to climb in (I managed to avoid the rust—good thing I wore my jeans), closed my door, got in, and drove off. Oh, that car coughed and wheezed like an old man with phlegm, but somehow we made it to the market.

"There are four basic ways to buy black-eyed peas," said Daddy as we walked toward the vegetable bins. I guess Yoda had begun the lesson. "In the stalk, out of the stalk, canned, and frozen." He walked me over to a big, free-standing bin of stalks. He took one in hands that trembled and shelled it smoothly. He picked up one and handed it to me. "Now you try," he said. I was amazed at how difficult it was.

"Our ancestors used to do this all day?" I grunted.

"This and more. Remind me one day to tell you about my cotton-picking days."

"You picked cotton?" I asked, impressed. The things you learn about a man while shelling black-eyed peas.

"Yeah, I picked cotton and had to stand at the back of the bus. Now pay attention to what you're doing," he ordered.

I managed to get out a pea, but in the process broke a nail. "Damn!" I said, putting my finger in my mouth. I paid thirty bucks for that nail.

"C'mon," he said. "I just wanted you to get a feel for the way the peas come in nature. Since we ain't got all day for all that's involved in the preparation of fresh peas, we're going to buy the kind that's already shelled. We'll get a pound of them."

"What about canned or frozen?" You would have thought I had just called him out of his name. He looked up at the ceiling, then over to an elderly woman who had been watching us closely.

"Where did I go wrong?" he asked her. She squinted, then laughed at his distress. I just stood there looking like an idiot.

"Don't feel bad," she told him. "Mine don't know nothing neither."

My father led me to the packaged-goods section. He told me this was a major compromise, buying black-eyed peas packaged up instead of fresh, but there wasn't enough time to do it to perfection. Sacrifices would have to be made. That was life.

Hell, canned peas would have been fine with me.

We also bought onions, carrots, celery, and tomato sauce. I put my foot down when he put a slab of salt pork in the cart. "Daddy, that's a heart attack waiting to happen! I can't believe you're still eating that mess!" The meat looked fatty, white, and crystalline. It scared me. I could feel the evil energy just pouring out of it. I recoiled in horror.

"It ain't real black-eyed peas without the salt pork, girl." Standoff in the meat section.

"I would prefer if we didn't use any meat at all, but let's compromise and use smoked turkey, okay?" Bravely, I replaced the hog with some good-sized smoked-turkey wings. Daddy glared at me as if to say how dare you, but I stood my ground. "Didn't the doctor tell you to lay off the salt and the meat?" He didn't reply, just glared. "Daddy, your high blood pressure, remember? Who's going to fuss at us if you get sick? Who's going to take care of us?" I wanted to say the word "love" but I didn't want him to have a stroke. Besides, he knew I was telling him how much I loved him. He relaxed and said, "C'mon, let's pay for this stuff." He al-

29

ready had a good supply of spices in his kitchen, so we headed for home.

As we put up the groceries, Daddy said with an awkward gentleness, "Donna, I know you're wondering why I made such a big fuss out of buying those black-eyed peas, but you need to know how important the beginning is to how the dish turns out in the end. If you don't take care in the beginning to choose your ingredients well, you're going to end up with a mess on your hands. Always take your time. Use the freshest produce, if you can. Shoot, grow your own. A good beginning will guarantee a good dish."

As our heroine putters around the kitchen, she reflects on the importance of beginning a project well. The principle applies to everything—business start-ups, social movements, baby making. God took his time in the Beginning, and look at how the universe turned out. Not bad!

World Up!

P. K. McCary

Now when the Almighty was first down with His program, He made the heavens and the earth. The earth was a fashion misfit, being so uncool and dark, but the Spirit of the Almighty came down real tough, so that He simply said, "Lighten up!" And that light was right on time. And the Almighty liked what He saw and let the light hang out a while before it was dark again. He laid out a name for the light, calling it "day" time and the dark He called "night" time so that all around it made up the first day.

The Almighty's program continued, making those dark ugly masses separate so that they made up the skies above and the big waters, oceans, below. And all was happenin' (the sky above, you see, and the oceans below), creating day two.

The Almighty hung tough with His program and commanded that the waters "Get to one place," and there was land and this He called earth. The water left, He called "seas."

And He was happy.

Then He commanded the earth to be down with every kind of grass, fruit- and plant-producin' tree which was like itself, and the earth was down enough to make the Almighty smile. Count 'em up, now—day three. So, the Almighty's program continued with bright lights which lit up the world at His command. The day differed from night 'round the clock, "twenty-four/seven"—turning weeks into months and months into "seasons," which make up years. And it was so.

The Almighty made two big lights and they did shine on the earth. The big light He called the sun and it rested itself over the earth during the day, and the little light, which He called the moon, cruised through the night. The Almighty added little lights called stars and put them in the sky and they did their share of lighting, so that now we have a day and a night for real and the Almighty was feeling mighty fine on the fourth day.

The Almighty then said, "I want the waters to have fish and other kinds of things and I want birds that fill the sky." And He made all them different kinds of living sea things and blessed them. And on the real tip, the Almighty commanded them to "Increase and fill up them waters," and the birds He commanded, "Multiply and fly the earth." And all was done by day five.

Now the Almighty was on the one with his program, replenishing the earth with every kind of animal—cattle and other creeping crawly things, reptiles and so on, and all the beasts like themselves, they were down with the program, too. It just so happened that the Almighty knew His stuff. And He was down with it all, duplicating things and all, and like Hisself He was together with the male; but male and female did He make.

And the Almighty was righteous by them and commanded them to, "Get down with My program and you will multiply and expand right here on the earth." Each living creature would be on the oneness with the birds and fish and all the animals. He admonished each of them to be hip to the fact that "These plants will hang tough with fruit for plenty of good eating." He was on the up-and-up with everything He had made and took care of what was His.

And the Almighty looked at things on His program, liked what He saw and when the nighttime was down again, it was the sixth day.

THE BEGINNING OF MAN

The Almighty finally finished making the earth and was right on target with all that He had made. So on the big seven, the Almighty said,

"Enough!" And the Almighty caused this day to be a special day 'cuz this was the day He'd finished His program.

And this was what went down with the Almighty's program. Now at first things hadn't been too cool 'cuz plants didn't grow with no H_2O 'round and there was no one hip to plant raising. But suddenly there was this mist that came from the ground and it watered down the earth, every square inch. And the Almighty created the brother from the dust of the ground and breathed heavily through his nose so that the brother was all the way live; and the brother became a human being.

The Almighty, He made a garden on the east side of Eden and the brother's crib was there and all. And the plants and trees that were good to look at grew. The Tree of Life grew, too, right in the heat of the garden (this was the tree 'tween bad and good). A river from Eden went around watering down the garden and then it divvied up into four parts.

The Almighty made the brother get down with his gig and take care of the garden. And the brother was told he could munch on every tree in the garden. "But be cool 'round the tree of knowledge. Please don't eat from it or you'll die."

And the Almighty felt it wasn't cool for the brother to be by hisself. "I'll make him someone to keep time with," God said. So he started form- ing every kind of animal out of the ground and brought 'em around to Adam (that was the brother's name) to see what he'd name them. And the brother was down with some great names for the animals, but he was still lonely. So the Almighty put the brother deep in a coma and took out a rib and sealed the place up again. And from the rib He created a sister and brought her down to the brother.

"Right-on," said Adam. "This is my woman, 'cuz she's part of me, the man." And that's why she's called woman, 'cuz she was made from the rib of man. And this is also why when a brother and sister get together he leaves his mother and father and belongs to her. The brother and sister weren't hip to the fact that they didn't have no clothes on neither, so this didn't faze them.

When Souls Were Made
Zora Neale Hurston

I thought about the tales I had heard as a child. How even the Bible was made over to suit our vivid imagination. How the devil always outsmarted God and how that over-noble hero Jack or John—not *John Henry*, who occupies the same place in Negro folk-lore that Casey Jones does in white lore and if anything is more recent—outsmarted the devil. Brer Fox, Brer Deer, Brer 'Gator, Brer Dawg, Brer Rabbit, Ole Massa and his wife were walking the earth like natural men way back in the days when God himself was on the ground and men could talk with him. Way back there before God weighed up the dirt to make the mountains. When I was rounding Lily Lake I was remembering how God had made the world and the elements and people. He made souls for people, but he didn't give them out because he said:

"Folks ain't ready for souls yet. De clay ain't dry. It's de strongest thing Ah ever made. Don't aim to waste none thru loose cracks. And then men got to grow strong enough to stand it. De way things is now, if Ah give it out it would tear them shackly bodies to pieces. Bimeby, Ah give it out."

So Folks went round thousands of years without no souls. All de time de soul-piece, it was setting 'round covered up wide God's loose raiment. Every now and then de wind would blow and hist up de cover and then de elements would be full of lightning and de winds would talk. So people told one 'nother that God was talking in de mountains.

De white man passed by it way off and he looked but he wouldn't go close enough to touch. De Indian and de Negro, they tipped by cautious too, and all of 'em seen de light of diamonds when de wins shook de cover, and de wind dat passed over it sung songs. De Jew come past and heard de song from de soul-piece then he kept on passin' and all of a sudden he grabbed up de soul-piece and hid it under his clothes, and run off down de road. It burnt him and tore him and throwed him down and lifted him up and toted him across de mountain and he tried to break loose but he couldn't do it. He kept on hollerin' for help but de rest of 'em run hid 'way from him. Way after while they come out of holes and corners and picked up little chips and pieces that fell back on de ground. So God mixed it up wide feelings and give it out to 'em. 'Way after while when He ketch dat Jew, He's goin' to 'vide things up more ekal.

Session Nine
Estella Conwill Majozo

I went in for an ultrasound. No, I didn't bring the pictures, but it was better than the movie 2010. My mother went in with me. This was the second one, you know. . . . Yes, the first one was some months ago. I went in and was stretched out on the table, right? We couldn't see anything at first then there on the screen was this tiny circular mass of baby and at its center was this dot—dancing wildly pomp-pomp-pomppomp . . . a cosmic pulsation . . . pulling everything in the room into its rhythm . . . yes, uh-huh, and what's almost as wild is this. It took me time to know exactly what it was that I was seeing, but what showed up on that screen— the baby . . . the circle with a dot in the center—is the ancient African symbol for everlasting life. Can you imagine? I guess you don't have to any more . . . something our people knew symbolically—something that was revealed centuries ago—shows up on this scientific screen in reality. This time, my mother and I could make out the baby's head and his little body and we kept looking and there from the blurred mass of body rose up his hand—this little little hand—reaching out to us. My mother reached back out to the little finger on the screen. We laughed! It was what Michelangelo tried to capture in his painting where God's hand reaches out to touch life into Adam . . . it's what they tried to get going with the movies *ET* (raising her finger in the air). Eat your heart out Steven Spielberg!

... and pregnancy—pregnancy itself—imagine that ... a symbol of love ... that's got to be what love is. I mean for men and for women—pregnancy—lending energy and strength—carrying another inside of you—becoming food ... giving nourishment from your very being towards the transformation and life of another ... and all the while ... all the while believing in the inexhaustible source of Divine Life.

Ultimate Frontier

Ari Brown

When music is true to a musician's voice, then his or her songs will be honest. Honesty is missing in a lot of our music today. It takes a lot of courage to play true to your soul. People might not like it. They may reject the message and the messenger. You might go hungry for a while. I think it was that fear of rejection that almost kept me from taking the biggest risk of my music career two decades ago.

During the late 1970s, I was playing sax at the Back Room, a jazz club in Chicago. Chicago was comfortable, it was cool. Maybe too comfortable. It was around this time that a great musician named Elvin Jones came to town. As fate would have it, his saxophone player abruptly left the band because of a family crisis. A friend told Elvin about me, and later, I was invited to sit in with the band.

About two weeks later, Elvin's wife and manager, Keiko Jones, called me and asked if I wanted to play with the band. This was a really big step for me. Actually, I was really scared because when you are playing you never know what your abilities are. You're comfortable playing in a familiar situation, but when you leave your safety net, you never know how people will respond to your music.

Anyway, I stalled while on the phone with Keiko. I made up this story about having another responsibility and promised to call her back. I could tell she was upset. After all, she had believed that I really wanted this opportunity.

After hanging up with her, I immediately phoned my friend and mentor, Rubin Cooper, Jr. He said, "Whatever you do in Chicago won't be worth half the work you'll do with Elvin Jones." So after his pep talk I called Keiko back and explained that I'd taken care of everything and was ready to go. Fortunately, she accepted me, fears and all.

The next week I flew to New York and rehearsed. That was my introduction to playing with Elvin Jones. During the following two years we performed twenty or thirty times in Europe, as well as other countries, such as Japan.

This experience furthered my career because it exposed me not only to a broader national audience, but also to my first international audience. It also did a lot for my performance because it gave me greater confidence. Initially, I was worried about whether or not my music would have the same impact on people who didn't know me as with those who were familiar with my work. The question was answered; I discovered that music was of the soul. If you're sincere about what you're doing, people will embrace you. I was able to transfer my same vibration from Chicago to New York to the world.

Because I took that scary first step, I learned that wherever I play, I can reach the hearts and minds of people from all walks of life, and that's a great accomplishment. My latest CD, *Ultimate Frontier*, is a testimony to my development as a musician. At the same time, I continue to grow. I'm constantly being challenged to be better. I've learned that the ultimate frontier is really myself. As long as I play my music in my own voice, I'll create new beginnings for myself, pave my own direction.

How to Grow a Business and a Family for Love, Livelihood, and the Revolution

Chavunduka and Steve Cobb

Our story is really two stories intertwined. It is the story of two independent, socially conscious musician-entrepreneurs who came together to make music. Our story is also about a marriage of not only two adults, but of eight prepubescent and adolescent people. Our relationship has been a grand social experiment. We are a tribe, a ready-made clan. We are thirteen strong now, a bonded family of eight children ages twenty-four down to six, a grandmother, an uncle, and a brother-in-law. Somehow we manage to make it work with a lot of give and take on both our parts.

We had known each other for years before we first came together romantically. Chavunduka was a single parent of sons ages thirteen and eight. Steve had a son, fourteen, and a daughter, six, who were not living with him. As musicians, we'd even worked gigs together (Cha sings; Steve plays drums, percussion, and guitar). We had never considered each other as love interests, but we both were looking for love and had experienced enough to know what we needed (and didn't need) in a relationship.

One day we both found ourselves working a wedding reception, of all things. After playing a set, we decided to slow dance and soon found ourselves trying to have a relationship. From that dance on, we spent lots of time together planning, talking, and learning to accept each other. On weekends, to facilitate child care during Steve's late-night gigs, we unintentionally experimented with living together.

During the trials of our courtship, we also experimented with collaborative music projects. We were both headed in similar directions (we were producing independent recordings); thus we agreed to combine our resources and energy. One of us headed our own record label, the other a music production company. We were very cautious. We had each been working on our music careers before we met and were somewhat afraid of losing autonomy. But we pushed forward. Our initial collaborations were benefit concerts for the United Negro College Fund. Our first event was small and fairly successful. However, the next one nearly ruined our health and finances. We lost nearly $10,000, Steve developed a hyperthyroid condition, and Cha, pregnant throughout the ordeal, experienced morning, afternoon, and evening sickness. One of our most vivid memories of that period was of a late night "supper" at Kentucky Fried Chicken. We had been beating the pavement and passing out flyers. We were so hungry, but we could only afford one teeny, tiny chicken sandwich, which we shared. It was a bittersweet moment filled with intense love, commitment, hope, and fear. For years, we have tried to find the lesson in that traumatic experience. We now believe that it was the challenge that showed us what we were made of; it also cemented our bond.

We were tested even further when we married and moved our families into one household. Initially, our plan was to maintain two separate but closely located residences. A first-floor—second-floor relationship. Yes, we were very cautious. It didn't work, of course. We enjoyed being together too much.

But ours was not the typical marriage. Steve's not the typical husband. Cha's not the typical wife. First, there was a ready-made family of eight with an addition on the way. And to further complicate things we were both creative people, performing artists, with no steady income. We were entrepreneurs juggling our businesses, careers, and domestic life on this same groove. Unpredictable schedules and paychecks, eight personalities and a brand-new relationship—it's a wonder we made it, but with the support of a great mom/landlady, we at least had a place to live.

We struggled through issues of love, respect, trust, responsibility, discipline, household order, economics, spirituality, ideology, occupation, parenting techniques, personal space, his past, her past, our future, and that of our children, knowing that for us and our community, the way we handled these challenges would represent a micro-example of the Black family's macro-possibilities.

In spite of our lofty ideals, there was often low-grade silent competition and the desire to be crowned the most learned, correct, and wisest in all areas of living. Having grown up in different types of households, we each constantly compared and struggled to prove that his parent/her parent was correct in his/her childrearing practices. *"I turned out okay, didn't I?"* We realized at some point that it was the values of our upbringing (if not the practices) that we shared.

Our sons went through an intense sibling rivalry, which made the early days quite interesting, but they managed to establish a respect for each other that eventually grew into a bond. We were rarely required to intervene, as they were quite adept in shaping their relationships and carving their spaces, the older brothers coaching the younger. When the teenage daughter decided to come and live with us, yet another dynamic was added. Although we got along, the who-knows-the-most-the-best contest persisted. A lot of family meetings were held to discuss the concerns of the day, mostly revolving around household order, food (*"Who drank all the juice?"*), and invasions of personal space, usually Cha's. We were very fortunate in that no one in the family enjoyed conflict. So we were pretty careful in choosing our words and relied heavily on Steve's favorite counsel, "Never attack."

We also gave birth, at home, to a new baby girl. She knew her mission. It was to unite her family inextricably. We called her Mpatanishi, peacemaker. The whole family participated in the birthing process, and we were connected forever.

It was during this time that Steve, having performed locally as a sideman, was called upon again to tour nationally. He rejoined Ramsey Lewis's group and traveled extensively—Japan, Europe, the Caribbean, and all over the United States. The impact on the family was manyfold. Financially speaking, the gig was a godsend. It was a semipredictable paycheck. It also provided great exposure and access for Steven, and hence our company. On the other hand, it often required single-parent management of our large, booming household. Steven often missed important family occasions, including the birth of our second child. The long-distance bills were large, and even though we missed each other tremendously, adjusting to being together became more difficult after each trip. Issues around personal space and autonomy kept coming up.

Although there was never a big blowup, there came a critical moment when we considered and discussed not being together. We even went so far as conceptualizing the division of our meager assets. We were tired. It was too hard. Too many people and personalities to deal with. Not enough money. There was frequent tension between us concerning the division of labor.

One night we discussed our dilemma as we sat parked in front of the house in our van (some of our best communication has occurred in that van). We spoke honestly and heatedly about our unmet expectations and the frustrations of our lives. We discovered that we both felt stuck, locked in, and obligated to perform in ways that we just couldn't. At that moment of simple and complete understanding, we released each other. We forgave each other and ourselves for having those feelings, because in spite of them, we were doing our best to do the right thing by each other and all of the children. We accepted that we each had the right to leave if we could not be happy and fulfilled. It was a liberating acceptance. For some reason, knowing that we had a choice freed our spirits and gave us a renewed supply of relationship energy.

So we carried forth with new projects, gradually merging our vision and revamping our strategy. The breakthrough occurred in 1992. It happened through the writing and recording of a new song, "It's Kwanzaa Time." The collective songwriting and production process verified a few things. We became very clear about our music business philosophy. Our mission was not only to create positive music, but also to build institutions that would serve to develop our culture and motivate our people. It was also clear that to do this we'd both have to work at it full-time. Steven was still on the road with Ramsey, and schedule conflicts began to develop. If we had a gig, Ramsey would undoubtedly have one on the same date. Although Steve's tenure with Ramsey's band ended as the result of a difference of opinion, Steve's decision was made easier knowing that his full energies could be devoted to our growing business.

The single release, "It's Kwanzaa Time," had grown into *Seven Principles*, our new compact-disc recording. It was the first contemporary collection of songs for Kwanzaa. Now we had a calling card. Television programs were interested, newspapers wanted stories, and teachers wanted us in their classrooms.

As we plunged deeper into the world of do-it-yourself music, we discovered that we could do much more. We learned new skills and honed old ones—computer-assisted music production, sales, program development, workshop facilitation, book publishing, graphic design, public relations, and more. With the support of our children and our village (relatives, friends, our children's teachers), we were able to travel across the country, performing at festivals, universities, and community events. It was hard work, but it gave us a pathway to the future and multiplied our possibilities.

The children involved themselves in our projects both on stage and behind the scenes. Although they would never admit it (they love to taunt us about our "lucrative" career choice), they were inspired by our boldness and tenacity. (It didn't hurt to see themselves mentioned in the media occasionally, either.) We amazed ourselves. We wore a lot of hats, and even with our own disorganized method, got a lot done.

The saga continues. These days we disagree (ever so slightly) about everything, but then we'll laugh and agree that it must be a phase. We still have problems with household order, sibling rivalry, and personal space, but since the household is now decreasing in size, we're hoping for a decrease in anxiety. So far, Ahkinyala, Gwinyayi, and Weusi have graduated from college; Chimu and Joshua are currently enrolled; Jeremiah is a high school scholar; and Mpatanishi and Zenzile (yeah, we had another sweet girl) brighten our every moment with their talent and zest for life.

Our business still calls on us to be brave and have faith, but it sustains us. We haven't "made it" yet, but having redefined success for ourselves, we are finding that the joy is in the journey.

The Darkness of Space Produced Life

Honorable Elijah Muhammad

If we see that One emerged out of all this darkness, what force or power in the darkness brought It out? One could not have come out of darkness unless force was in the darkness to bring It out. In the Universe now there is a force that moves seemingly unmovable Stars. After so long and so long, the Star which we saw here at this point has moved over here to another point. If that Star moves over here to another point within 10, 20, 30, 40, 50, 100, or a thousand years, force made it move. It could not move alone.

So this teaches us Brother and Sister (you go back and get your scientist and I will contend with him and he will contend with Me) that the force of the space which seemingly looks as though it is nothing, has the power to bring up objectives that are hidden in it to our view. We don't wind up the Universe and tell her to bring Jupiter over to us. No. Jupiter is moving by force. We don't say to a Star that is a hundred trillion miles or further back there, "Come out and show us yourself." There is already a force that is going to bring it to our view.

The One was already in the darkness but could not be given to us until the Time brought It about. Then when the Time brought It about, It emerged in our view into a revolving Life that was hidden in the dark-

46

ness. We don't know how many trillions of years It was there, but It was there. It made Itself out of a fine Atom of water that It found out there with It in the darkness of the Universe. We could not see Life emerging out of space without water because we can't produce Life without water. Therefore, there is some water out there in that darkened world (space). This space has produced us Life, but how long was that Life out there before it produced us a form? You calculate how long.

If One emerged out of this Black darkness and started the Black darkness moving, with power that the Black darkness can use itself in calculating time, this is a Wise God. Don't play with Him. So, just imagine that we are looking at the darkness in space and here is One coming out of space, out of that Black darkness. How did He produce Himself, teach Himself to talk, walk, preach and sing?

What is Earth made out of? The Earth is a ball of what looks like finely ground stone. It has great stones supporting those little fine stones. What did God mean, other than His people, when He said "Can you count the grains of sand on the seashore, Abraham?" Now the number of His people could not be counted, but why did He point out this sand on the seashore? It was not because Abraham could not count them but because Abraham must learn whose gigantic mill ground those sands down there. Somebody put them, down there. They are beautiful and someone made them. After Abraham had known the grains of sand He could ask him, "Who made them?" But Abraham was far from being that type of mathematician to be able to calculate how many grains had been laid down there on the seashore.

The figures one (1) and six (6) are the most outstanding figures we have. One represents the God that Created the Heavens and the Earth and the other one represents the same, the "6." Why is that? He didn't stop growing! He grew into the scientific knowledge of "6" and when He got into the number "6" He still had us puzzled. We didn't know how to overtake Him because the "6" came 6 trillion years after the "1" (from the year "1") and we can hardly count into 6,000 years.

Birth Pains of the Civil Rights Movement

Rosa Parks and E. D. Nixon

On December 1, 1955, Mrs. Rosa L. Parks was arrested for violating the bus-segregation ordinance in Montgomery, Alabama. She refused to get up out of her seat for a white rider because, as she has often said, "My feet hurt." Contrary to popular belief that this was one isolated incident, Rosa Parks says that "I had almost a life history of being rebellious against being mistreated because of my color." Although no one could have predicted that moment on the bus, Rosa Parks's "life history" had prepared her for it. Her one small act of defiance launched the Montgomery Bus Boycott and the civil rights movement was in full swing. The following are oral histories from Howell Raines's My Soul Is Rested: The Story of the Civil Rights Movement. Rosa Parks and E. D. Nixon, who was the state NAACP president, regional officer of the Brotherhood of Sleeping Car Porters, and Mrs. Parks's boss at the time, were interviewed.

ROSA PARKS: I had had problems with bus drivers over the years, because I didn't see fit to pay my money into the front and then go around to the back. Sometimes bus drivers wouldn't permit me to get on the bus, and I had been evicted from the bus. But as I say, there had been incidents over the years. One of the things that made this get so much publicity was the fact the police were called in and I was placed under arrest. See, if I had just been evicted from the bus and he hadn't placed me under arrest or had any charges brought against me, it probably could have been just another incident.

I had left my work at the men's alteration shop, a tailor shop in the Montgomery Fair department store, and as I left work, I crossed the street to a drugstore to pick up a few items instead of trying to go directly to the bus stop. And when I had finished this, I came across the street and looked for a Cleveland Avenue bus that apparently had some seats on it. At that time it was a little hard to get a seat on the bus. But when I did get to the entrance to the bus, I got in line with a number of other people who were getting on the same bus.

As I got up on the bus and walked to the seat I saw there was only one vacancy that was just back of where it was considered the white section. So this was the seat that I took, next to the aisle, and a man was sitting next to me. Across the aisle there were two women, and there were a few seats at this point in the very front of the bus that was called the white section. I went on to one stop and I didn't particularly notice who was getting on the bus, didn't particularly notice the other people getting on. And on the third stop there were some people getting on, and at this point all of the front seats were taken. Now in the beginning, at the very first stop I had got on the bus, the back of the bus was filled up with people standing in the aisle and I don't know why this one vacancy that I took was left, because there were quite a few people already standing toward the back of the bus. The third stop is when all the front seats were taken, and this one man was standing and when the driver looked around and saw he was standing, he asked the four of us, the man in the seat with me and the two women across the aisle, to let him have those front seats.

At his first request, didn't any of us move. Then he spoke again and said, "You'd better make it light on yourselves and let me have those seats." At this point, of course, the passenger who would have taken the seat hadn't said anything. In fact, he never did speak, to my knowledge. When the three people, the man who was in the seat with me and the two women, stood up and moved into the aisle, I remained where I was. When the driver saw that I was still sitting there, he asked if I was going to stand up. I told him, no, I wasn't. He said, "Well, if you don't stand up, I'm going to have you arrested." I told him to go on and have me arrested.

He got off the bus and came back shortly. A few minutes later, two policemen got on the bus, and they approached me and asked if the driver had asked me to stand up, and I said yes, and they wanted to know why I didn't. I told them I didn't think I should have to stand up. After I had paid my fare and occupied a seat, I didn't think I should have to give it up. They placed me under arrest then and had me get in the police car, and I was taken to jail and booked on suspicion, I believe. The questions were asked, the usual questions they ask a prisoner or somebody that's under arrest. They had to determine whether or not the driver wanted to press charges or swear out a warrant, which he did. Then they took me to jail and I was placed in a cell. In a little while I was taken from the cell, and my picture was made and fingerprints taken. I went back to the cell then, and a few minutes later I was called back again, and when this happened I found out that Mr. E. D. Nixon and Attorney and Mrs. Clifford Durr had come to make bond for me.

In the meantime before this, of course . . . I was given permission to make a telephone call after my picture was taken and fingerprints taken. I called my home and spoke to my mother on the telephone and told her what had happened, that I was in jail. She was quite upset and asked me had the police beaten me. I told her, no, I hadn't been physically injured, but I was being held in jail, and I wanted my husband to come and get me out. . . . He didn't have a car at that time, so he had to get someone to bring him down. At the time when he got down, Mr. Nixon and the Durrs had just made bond for me, so we all met at the jail and we went home. . . .

E. D. NIXON: Then we went on up to the house and I said to Mrs. Parks, "Mrs. Parks"—her mother had some coffee made—I said, "Mrs. Parks, this is the case we've been looking for. We can break this situation on the bus with your case."

She said, "Well, I haven't thought of it just like that." So we talked to her mother and her husband, and finally they came 'round, said they'd go along with it.

She said, "All right." She said, "You know, Mr. Nixon, if you say so, I'll go along with it."

I said, "Okay, we can do it."

What was there about Mrs. Parks that made her the right litigant as opposed to these others?

Mrs. Parks was a married woman. She had worked for me for twelve years, and I knew her. She was morally clean, and she had a fairly good academic training. Now, she wasn't afraid and she didn't get excited about anything. If there ever was a person that we woulda been able to break the situation that existed on the Montgomery city line, Rosa L. Parks was the woman to use. And I knew that. I probably woulda examined a dozen more before I got there if Mrs. Parks hadn't come along before I found the right 'un. 'Cause, you see, it's hard for you to see it, it's hard for the average person—it's hard for the black people here in Montgomery to see. It's hard for a whole lot of people far away from here to see it. But when you have set 'cross the table and talked with black people in investigations as long as I have over a period of years, you just know it. . . . Well, I spent years in it and I knew it . . . when I selected Mrs. Parks, that was the person.

And so after we agreed, oh, I guess we spent a couple of hours discussing this thing. Then I went home and I took a sheet of paper and I drew right in the center of the paper. I used that for the square and then I used Hunter Station, Washington Park, Pickett Springs, all the different areas in Montgomery, and I used a slide rule to get a estimate. I discovered nowhere in Montgomery at that time a man couldn't walk to work if he wanted to. I said, "We can beat this thing."

I told my wife about it and I said, "You know what?"

She said, "What?"

I said, "We're going to boycott the buses."

She said, "Cold as it is?"

I said, "Yeah."

She said, "I doubt it."

I said, "Well, I'll tell you one thing. If you keep 'em off when it cold, you won't have no trouble keeping 'em off when it get hot."

She shook her head. She said, "My husband! If headaches were selling for a dollar a dozen, my husband would be just the man to walk in the drugstore and say, 'Give me a dozen headaches.' " [Laughs]

So anyhow, I recorded quite a few names, starting off with Rev. Abernathy, Rev. Hubbard, Rev. King, and on down the line, and I called some of the people who represent people so that they could get the word out. The first man I called was Reverend Ralph Abernathy. He said, "Yes, Brother Nixon, I'll go along. I think it's a good thing."

The second person I called was the late Reverend H. H. Hubbard. He said, "Yes, I'll go along with you."

And I called Rev. King, was number three, and he said, "Brother Nixon, let me think about it awhile, and call me back."

When I called him back, he was number nineteen, and of course, he agreed to go along. I said, "I'm glad you agreed, because I already set the meeting up to meet at your church."

One Drop Can Change an Ocean
Mary T. Carr

Several years ago I realized that I was not cut out for the nine-to-five grind. I would work hard and even get promoted, but after four or five years, I'd get restless and move on. I decided to quit Corporate America for good and become my own boss. With my husband supporting me every step of the way, I began to work in my basement as a hairstylist.

I loved my new profession! Not only could I set my own schedule, I enjoyed the interaction with my clients. I learned to listen to their problems and, in many cases, actually helped to inspire them. I'd lay hands on their scalps and minister to their souls. Gradually I realized I was being called to the ministry. I enrolled in seminary and studied extensively to fulfill the position in ministry for which I was called.

My first love in church was the youth, especially older teens. We went on trips, church conventions, and other activities. I convened rap sessions in which young people could speak freely about all the things that were troubling them—violence, substance abuse, peer pressure, teen pregnancy, and more. Our sessions became quite popular. The young people would tell their friends about them and, as a result, the youth department grew by leaps and bounds.

Unfortunately, as is often the case when you become successful at a thing, members of the church became jealous of my popularity with the young people. One of the senior ministers even felt threatened! I was put in another position, but by then, nothing could stop the young people's excitement—not petty adult jealousy or the church's lack of support. Under the leadership of another minister, I continued my work with youth until I went out on my own.

My ministry began in the basement of my home with five people, including my husband. We prayed and invited others to join in. Consequently, the ministry began to grow. Soon, we needed a bigger place to serve the people and also work in the community. I have been offered more lucrative positions, but I've chosen to work in underserved, neglected African American communities and with people who have lost control of their lives. This kind of ministry requires an army of sorts, so I began to train others to work with me. We developed strategies that enabled us to touch the lives of those who were hurting, disenfranchised, dispossessed, and inundated with problems. Our family started to grow. People were coming into our fellowship, learning how to lead and building character and self-esteem.

Inevitably, I returned my attention to the youth, for it is the youth in these impoverished communities who are suffering the most. Many have to walk convoluted routes to school just to avoid gang territories. The schools and neighborhoods in which they attempt to learn and live are like war zones or prisons.

Many of the children are doing poorly in school and their parents cannot afford private tutors. Dropout rates are high. Most of these children are not bad, just unprepared for school and embarrassed at their inability to understand class material. I decided to create an afterschool tutoring program for the children in the community.

Eight years ago, I began this work with the children in my congregation, helping them with their homework on Wednesday evenings. As a result, the children's schoolwork improved, their self-confidence grew, and they were learning the importance of staying in school. Soon, the workload increased and help was needed. A brother in the congregation joined me, and we were on our way.

The following fall, we extended our schedule to Mondays, Tuesdays, and Wednesdays, from 3 to 6 P.M. More tutors were needed, so I began my search. It was long and tedious work, but it was worth seeing my dream of a free school that helped youth develop academically, socially, psychologically, and spiritually come to fruition. We named our program the Community Academic Paraschool (CAPS).

Three of us tutored the program voluntarily. There was no charge. We wanted this program to help low-income families who could not afford to pay for private tutoring. Since the high-achiever and "A" students did not necessarily need our services, we decided to cater to low achievers and students with little family support. We wanted to help students who were insecure and had low self-esteem, students who did not care whether they passed or failed.

In the beginning, we did not have a lot of equipment or materials, however, we learned to be creative. As the word got out, we received additional help, mostly financial support from private and institutional funders. Much of the money went toward paying our volunteer tutors stipends. Eventually we hired a program director to run the program.

I believe the reason for CAPS's success is that everyone in the program, from the tutors to the program director, is empowered to lead. From the beginning of this community-based ministry, I sought workers who were willing and able to take the reins. CEOs are not going to be around forever, and if their dreams are to stay alive, they should be willing to pass on their vision and knowledge so that those left behind can continue to grow and develop. The following are some of the things I've done to grow leaders:

1. **Build trust.** I allow people to see that I love and trust them. I tell them how important their creative talents are to the ministry and to themselves. Having confidence in the person you are training is very important because it helps the person develop confidence in him/herself.

2. **Delegate tasks.** I give people jobs to do, then I let them do it. I teach them to take risks, and I let them make mistakes. When problems arise, I ask: What did you learn from the experience? How can this experience help you improve the quality of your work?

3. **Build capacity.** I encourage people to give to the community and help someone else, without expecting payment. If we are to build our communities and help others, then we must be willing to give of ourselves.

How Sky and Earth Became One: A Yoruba Creation Story
Ralph Cheo Thurmon (Babaorisamola)

On creation eve, Obatala and Orunmilla sat in the perfect light of the sky as they looked down at the earth, into the mysterious and dark domain of the sea goddess, Olokun. Obatala sat on a throne made from a huge ivory elephant tusk; Orunmilla's throne, made from a kola nut, was trimmed with sixteen cowry shells. As they watched and waited and pondered the mystery of the sea, Obatala carved human figurines from the white wood of a tree found only in their father's garden.

Obatala dropped the figurines. One by one they fell through marshmallow clouds and splashed mightily into Olokun's great sea. Olokun accepted Obatala's gifts with a splash of salty sea on Obatala's feet. When his feet dried, Obatala scraped off the salt and shared it with the other Orisas in Orun, the dwelling place of the divine beings.

Obatala was a great artist, so his father Olorun often sent him to planets to mold and shape humans in the images of the different Orisas. Once created, Olorun would breathe life into the humans, and the Orisas would claim them as their children. The Orisas taught their human children the wisdom and power of earth and sky. And when the humans finished their earthly tasks, the Orisas showed them the way back home.

"Orunmilla," said Obatala, "look at the endless water and darkness on the earth. Even you have said that earth is a sore eye to the universe. Of all the millions of planets I've created, only earth remains empty, lifeless."

"Do you think the earth is ready for life?" asked Orunmilla.

Obatala shrugged. "Only Olorun can answer that question."

Obatala and Orunmilla assumed a meditative posture and contemplated the plight of earth for eternities. They waited for a message from Olorun.

Obatala uttered a secret prayer to Olorun, and at that moment, Orunmilla opened his left hand, then the right one. Obatala smiled at the sign. Olorun had granted him his desire to make earth a livable planet.

Early the next day at Orunmilla's house, Agemo, the chameleon-servant to Olorun, crawled inside and announced that his master had sent him to assist Obatala in his earth mission. Close behind Agemo was Esu, the master linguist and divine trickster. Esu was the youngest of all the Orisas, and his antics helped make everyday life in Orun unpredictable and interesting.

Esu said, "Olorun has sent me to remove uncertainty from your journey to earth." Obatala and Orunmilla welcomed Esu. "My brothers, let's go outside and dance the Dance of Ifa to divine what Olorun would have Obatala take on his journey to earth."

Obatala agreed. As they all went outside, Esu laughed. Esu's laughter was like the roar from a herd of lions. All of Orun was awakened by the sound. The Orisas knew that when Esu laughs something interesting must be going on, so they came and formed a circle around Obatala, Orunmilla, Agemo, and Esu. Orunmilla began to dance.

His movements were careful and deliberate, and soon he began to receive answers from Olorun. As Orunmilla danced and reported what he received, Obatala recorded the message. Four things would be needed for the journey to earth: a chain of gold long enough to reach earth, a snail shell with enough dry soil to cover the waters, a white hen to spread the soil, and a palm nut to quench Obatala's thirst.

The task fell upon Agemo to gather the needed things. He found everything but the chain of gold.

"I will go and get gold pieces and have the chain made," said Esu. First he held out his hands to the Orisas, who gave fully of all the gold they had. They were happy to give because they knew that in return, Olorun would answer the prayers and offerings of their children on the different planets. Then Esu went collecting gold all over Orun. When he had enough, he took the gold to a goldsmith, who, without pay, assembled the gold pieces into a magnificent chain.

With the white hen on his shoulder, the snail shell in his pocket, and the palm nut in his pouch, Obatala heaved the mighty chain over the side of the divine city. Down it stormed through the sky, through the clouds. Down it rained with thunder and gold lightening. As the chain fell to earth, Obatala began his downward descent.

Obatala climbed down for days. Finally, he made it to the end of the golden chain, but to his dismay, he realized that Esu had not collected enough gold to reach the earth. The chain was not long enough! Obatala clung fast as he looked down into Olokun's dim and marshy domain.

Orunmilla had been monitoring Obatala's descent, however, and rushed to help when he saw that his brother was in trouble. He sent a message over space and time to Obatala. Thank Olorun for Orunmilla! thought Obatala. He now knew what to do. Obatala took the snail shell out of his pocket and emptied the dry soil onto the earth. He then dispersed the dry soil across the great waters. The frenzied white hen was released to spread the soil unevenly in places. Mountains and valleys were formed. One such mountain touched the bottom of Obatala's feet. He let go of the chain and walked down the hill to the level earth. Obatala planted the palm nuts and the trees grew lush and wild.

Out of respect to Olokun, the hen had covered only a small portion of the earth with dry soil. Obatala offered Olokun palm wine and a gift of fine cloth from Olorun. The sea trembled, and a woman and man with fish-like bodies arose from the water. They waved and welcomed him. Their faces were indigo colored and glimmered like fine jewels.

"Good morning, Obatala, son of Olorun. Welcome to Ile Ife," said the two in unison.

Obatala bowed in greeting. "Olokun, we will never forget that the waters of the earth are your domain. Annually, gifts and offerings will be brought to this spot."

"Thank you, Obatala," said Olokun. "And I have a gift for you."

A great wave rolled to the seashore the figurines Obatala had carved and dropped from the sky.

Obatala was greatly moved. His children! How beautiful and full of potential they were! "Your children are endowed with wisdom and good character. They will multiply and create many more children. At the end of their earth journey, they will return to Orun," said Olokun.

The fish beings returned to the sea, and Obatala began his patient wait for the figurines to dry. For days and weeks he waited, but the figurines still dripped wet.

One day, Agemo descended the golden chain. Olorun had sent him to see how things were going. "Agemo, the earth is almost complete," said Obatala. "If I had light and warmth, the figurines would dry and Olorun could blow the breath of life into them."

Agemo returned to Orun to present Obatala's request to Olorun. Olorun granted Obatala's wish. He pinched light from Orun, rolled it into a sun, and placed it in the sky. The figurines began to dry in the sun.

While the figurines were drying, Obatala created more. There was none of the white wood from Olorun's garden, so Obatala took the clay from the earth and used it to create more humans.

Creation is a difficult task, and soon Obatala grew tired and thirsty. He tapped the palm tree and made palm wine. Obatala drank until he fell into a drunken stupor. Listless and hardly able to stand, he resumed working. As his unsteady hands worked the clay of the earth, he kept his eye, as much as the palm wine would allow, on the figurines he had carved in Orun, trying to emulate their perfection. Obatala finally looked to the sky and said to Olorun, "I have made humans. All they need now is the breath of life."

Olorun granted his faithful son's wish. The figurines became flesh, and blood ran warm in their veins. Obatala was happy. He drank more palm wine and called the Orisas from Orun to claim their children. He fell fast asleep.

When the Orisas came, they chose their children. They chose the strongest and the ablest of Obatala's creations. Some went with the Orisas to found other cities and nations, others were left with the sleeping Obatala as tribute. When Obatala woke the next morning, he was pleased to see his human children working to make a new city.

But as he looked more closely, Obatala noticed that some of the humans were awkwardly made. Some had one leg, others had none. Some had crooked limbs and hunch backs. Some were albinos, still others could not talk or hear. Every possible mistake that could be made with the creation of a human Obatala had made. For an eternity Obatala mourned. He made a pledge: "Never will I drink palm wine again. From this time on I will be the special protector of humans who have been created imperfectly."

Today, priests of Obatala wear only white cloth, grow a white beard, and are forbidden to drink palm wine out of respect to Obatala. They work to continue his legacy on earth as the protectors of humanity.

GLOSSARY

Orun—dwelling place of divine beings; also refers to "sky"

Orisas—divine beings

Obatala—Yoruba god of creation; son of Olorun

Olorun—God; owner of the sky; most high

Orunmilla—Yoruba deity of divination; the one who ascertains the mind of Olorun; son of Olorun

Olokun—Yoruba sea god

Agemo—messenger of Olorun

Esu—master linguist and divine trickster

STEP TWO

Sorting the Peas

After we put up the groceries, Daddy had me boil the turkey wings in a pot of water. "If you can boil hot dogs, you can boil turkey wings." Ha ha, very funny. "Set the timer for about an hour." I did.

Then he told me to get out the old blue porcelain mixing bowl he and my mother had received as a wedding present thirty-nine years ago. Funny how so many glasses and cups had broken over the years, but not the old mixing bowls.

"For a thick stew, we'll need about half the bag of peas," my father said, handing me the two-pound bag. While he spoke, he was reaching and stooping, collecting his tools, herbs, and spices we would need to make the peas.

"Empty half the bag of peas into the bowl," he said.

"Half? Shouldn't we measure it just to make sure?" I asked. Daddy looked to heaven.

"To make sure of what?" he asked. "That you don't get one more pea in the mix than the recipe calls for?"

"I just want to get it right," I said.

"You will, just trust yourself. Don't rely on what a recipe says, or even what I say." I raised my eyebrows. "Feel your way through the process."

Nervously, I emptied half the bag into the bowl, then held it up to determine if it was half full. If I had had a ruler I would have used it, but that was too anal even for me, so I plucked out five peas and threw them into the bowl. Satisfied that I had gotten pretty close to half the bag, I stood at attention and awaited further instructions. Daddy shook his head. Young people of today. He motioned me to the kitchen table and told me to have a seat. He set the bowl of peas in front of me. All those beady eyes, staring at me. They knew I didn't have a clue about what to do with them.

"Now, I want you to look through the peas and take all the rocks out."

"Rocks! Why'd they put rocks in the bag?"

Daddy sighed. "Black-eyed peas come from the ground, so what did you expect? I also want you to take out all the discolored ones." He picked up a pea and showed it to me. "This is a good pea. Anything that doesn't look like this, take it out."

I nodded, saluted, and commenced to sorting. Daddy turned on the radio. It was already tuned to his favorite blues and jazz station. Satchmo was singing in that famous gritty tenor, and my father was in heaven. He sat down, closed his eyes, and snapped his fingers.

With Daddy pacified for the moment and not looking over my shoulders, I relaxed and set about my task. My hands became coated with a thin layer of dust as I combed through the mound of peas with my fingers. I found tiny rocks and peas that looked grayish, which I took out and put to the side. I analyzed every pea in that bowl. And even though

Daddy didn't mention it, it occurred to me that I also needed to check for firmness. More peas were put to the side. I shook a few more loose from the bag to make up for the ones I had taken out.

After a few minutes, Daddy came over to inspect my work. "Good," he said. "You're doing good." I smiled, basking in his praise. My father was never one to hand out phoney compliments. When I was a little girl doing homework at this very same table, my father could make me wilt. Math homework in particular was torture. A high school teacher until the day he retired, Daddy was merciless when it came to us doing our homework and getting a good education. We preferred working with our mother because, though just as committed to education and also a teacher, she was a softer touch. Many a homework session with my father ended in tears. But when he'd praise me, I knew he meant it, and I'd bloom.

"How's your manuscript coming along?" he asked as I shifted, sorted, and analyzed.

"It's coming. I should be done by the end of the week," I said, irritated at the interruption. I needed to concentrate.

Amused, Daddy watched me. "Did I ever tell you about my early teaching days?" Irritated, I shook my head. He was going to tell me a story. Lovely. "I remember when I first started teaching. I had this dream that I wanted to save the poor kids in the ghetto. So I'd say to my students, Study hard! You don't want to stay in the ghetto all your lives, do you?

"One day, I guess they had had enough. A girl in my class told me, 'Mr. Williams, every day you tell us to study hard so we can get out of the ghetto, but you know what? My family lives in the ghetto, as you call it. All the people we love live in the ghetto. And even if we studied hard, graduated, got a good job, and moved out of the ghetto, where would we go? To the suburbs to live with the Ku Klux Klan?

"'Mr. Williams, wouldn't it be better if we studied hard, graduated, got a good job, and stayed right where we are? That way we could improve things.' Well, that made a lot of sense to me. That little girl taught me something that day. I didn't stop telling them to study hard and get a good job, but I did stop that get-out-of-the-ghetto nonsense. I relaxed, and it made all the difference in my relationship with my students. I even became a better teacher."

I looked up at my father. "Is there a moral to this story?"

"Yeah, I'm telling you to relax. Look at you: your face is all tight and your shoulders are all tense. Relax. It's just a bowl of black-eyed peas, okay?"

I had to laugh. I was approaching this task like life and death.

As Donna spends quality time with the peas in the bowl, she becomes wise to the ways of the pea—their proper color, texture, and size. She realizes that it takes wisdom to discern a rock from a pea. Rocks try to hide by camouflaging themselves, and the good cook learns to use sight, touch, even sound to sort them out. Donna relaxes; she realizes that experience is indeed the great teacher. Relaxation and observation have helped her to become wise in other areas of her life—relationships, career, child rearing—maybe the formula would help her to become a good cook as well.

Ritual

Iyanla Vanzant

Secret, sacred, words uttered in secret, sacred places teach you to honor yourself. Honoring what you feel when you are not quite sure what it is teaches you to trust yourself. Trusting yourself to do it when no one has told you that you can teaches you how Divine you actually are. Doing it the same way, at the same time, in the same place, even when you cannot see and do not know what will come of it, teaches you to honor and trust your divinity. That is what I call a ritual. An act that brings you face to face into a trusting and loving relationship with the divinity of your own Self.

Few of us are given the authority, opportunity or encouragement to be self-affirming. We are taught to do most things for the approval and acceptance of others. Our thoughts must manifest as actions that others will approve of and reward us for. We are encouraged to follow the "normal way" of doing things. The same way others are doing the same things. The covert message is that we are taught to compete with those who are doing what we are doing in an effort to do it better than they are. External standards, external approval, external acceptance leave little room for self-imposed standards of approval or acceptance. If we do it differently, others will not approve. If we create a new way, others become intimidated. We are taught to recognize and embrace what others say as sacred and what others do as sacred. The rituals we learn to embrace and perform derive their meaning from external factors, leaving little room for us to learn on our own the sacredness that creating personal rituals can offer.

I must admit, I have been afraid of the word and practice of *rituals*. Somewhere, somehow, I came to believe that ritual was a bad thing. Perhaps it was because I had been involved with rituals others had prescribed for me without ever being told that they were in fact rituals. Saturday shopping, Thursday washing, Sunday School and Friday night franks and beans were all rituals that gave meaning to my life. Perhaps it was the African phobia imparted to me by the many episodes of *Tarzan* I had seen. When I thought about the word, it sounded like magic. Magic is dark. Dark, magic rituals will send your soul straight to hell. I was not willing to risk that, so I dismissed my power to perform self-affirming rituals. I left my spiritual and emotional empowerment up to others without realizing I was even doing that in a very systematic and ritualistic manner.

I'm not sure she realizes it, but my grandmother taught me about the need and place of rituals in life. Every morning, my grandmother would get up, wash up, make a pot of coffee. She would then place a chair by the kitchen window and silently read from a small, frayed black book. I watched her when she thought I was asleep. I never questioned her because I somehow knew that what she was doing was sacred. The book she read was the Bible. Every morning she performed her personal prayer ritual. By 7 A.M., she was fully dressed, breakfast was ready, and my clothes were laid out for me to put on. It was more than just her responsibility as my primary caretaker. It was a morning ritual. Without an explanation as to why or what it meant, Grandma instructed me to get up, make by bed and be washed by 7:15. We were blessing our breakfast by 7:30. These were ritualistic acts that led to my sense of security as a child.

Every Monday Grandma and I washed the crystal knick-knacks and polished the silver. On Tuesday and Thursday, Grandma made my brother and me take Father John's and castor oil. On Thursday evening, we washed our socks and underwear by hand on the scrub board. We hung them up on a line in the bathroom and put them away when we came home from school on Friday. Every Saturday morning, Grandma would make me sprinkle Daddy's shirts and the pillow cases that she had washed. I rolled them up tightly, placed them in a plastic bag, and put them in the refrigerator. By 6 P.M. that evening, while we were watching *Howdy Doody* or *Captain Kangaroo*, the ironing ritual began. The ironing ritual was followed by memorizing certain Psalms or reciting, in order, sixty-six books of the Bible. Eating on time, going to bed on time, getting up according to Granny's rigid and strict schedule, were all rituals that I decided were too much for me to adhere to the day I turned sixteen.

Grandma paid her bills at the same time and on time every month. She never had a toothache and I don't think she ever had a cold. There was no dust in her house and her plants never died, especially that big, ugly snake plant that she kept right by the door. Grandma didn't know her birthday and she never went to school. How she read the Bible is still a mystery to me. She could not spell meditation but she did it every day, at the same time, in the same place. As a child watching her, I thought she was crazy. As an adult, having abandoned all the meaningless little acts that were part of childhood experience, poverty, confusion, and lack of purpose eventually brought me right back to where I started: creating order in my life through a structured, ritualistic way of doing things. The lack of structure, showing up as a bad marriage and mental and physical exhaustion, helped me to realize that Grandma's daily rituals, weekly, monthly rituals gave life a sense of order and meaning. In my rebellion against her and fear of the world, I abandoned rituals in order to go with the flow.

What Grandma did not give me and what I failed to pick up to until very late in life was the "rite" to create my own rituals. If there was no one in authority there to tell me how to do it, when to do it, or if I was doing it right, I shied away from the things called rituals. If it seemed like too much work and if it didn't seem to reap some tangible reward, I discounted the meaning of private, sacred, daily rituals. It never dawned on me until well into my adulthood that eating dinner every Sunday at 3 P.M. was a ritual. I did not understand that sitting between Grandma's legs every Sunday night to get my hair braided while watching Ed Sullivan was a ritual. Once I got the hang of it, I understood that flowing through self-created drama and crisis in the name of personal freedom was not all that it was cracked up to be. I needed the order, stability, and empowerment that self-created daily rituals offered.

Grandma called it "following God's clock," and she explained how the clock worked. The early-morning hours of the day were the best time to create the kind of day that you wanted to experience. The sunlight hours of the day were the best time to do the things that would bring to life the very things you wanted in your life. The darkness of the day was the time for you to revitalize yourself and make medicine. Every person has a sacred, secret medicine that helps them to function better during the day. That medicine could be a prayer or a special bath. It is best to take your medicine in the quiet of the night. "Those who pray in secret, God will reward openly!" Spring is the time for new growth and fresh starts. Start your new projects in the spring. Summer is the time that will bring the benefits of what you have done in the spring. You reap your just rewards in the summer. Fall is the time of death, eliminating the old, worn-out, and useless. Clean out, clear out, get rid of what is not working in the fall. Winter is the time to rest, rejuvenate, and plan what you will do in the spring. Slow down in the winter. Stay in during the winter. Get ready for what you want to do next in the winter. Grandma also said that the sun is the masculine energy, the energy that supports life. Do your work in the daylight. The moon is feminine energy, the energy in which life is created. Night is time to think, evaluate, and plan. She told me if I watched God's clock and lived according to it, I would always be on time and in time to do what I had come to life to do. What Grandma called "the clock" is what the ancient Africans call ritual. A time and place to do what needs to be done to reinforce yourself and your life.

In its purest form and most sacred sense, a ritual is a prescribed way of doing an act or series of acts with the intent to manifest a desired outcome. A ritual is a traditional or ceremonial approach to an event or series of events with a belief in the sacredness of the event. There are religious rituals like communion; social rituals like weddings; family rituals like Thanksgiving or Christmas dinner; and, there are personal rituals like bathing, shaving, praying, or having your hair done. These rituals create, utilize, and release energy. They order and structure your time and energy. They give rise to a personal sense of meaning and empowerment. They provide an opportunity to release the external and embrace the internal. They create and demand a sacred place in our hearts, minds, and lives.

All living beings have the "rite" to create sacred, personal rituals for themselves and in their lives. Others may not recognize them or appreciate them. Do not perform your rituals as a means to gain acceptance. Perform them to gain greater acceptance of yourself. Your personal rituals can be elaborate and time consuming or quick and to the point. What will give your rituals meaning is the intent you hold in your heart and mind. A personal ritual can strengthen you, cause you to focus, bring you peace or a sense of well-being. The most potent rituals are those which give you a sense of oneness and connection to yourself and your Highest Self. Learned rituals can be adapted to specific needs. New rituals can be created and expanded. The key is to know that your ritual is sacred and special for you. It is a means of honoring the divine energy of the Most High in your being. It is an opportunity for you to be with yourself and honor yourself. A ritual is something that you can do for yourself to remind yourself of just how blessed you really are.

Finding a Leg to Stand On

Dwight Anthony McKee

As Black women are waiting to exhale and Black men are struggling to get a breath at all, the dynamic of the Black male-female relationship has taken on a new, even more complicated significance. Competing against white women, jail cells, drugs, and sexually conflicted men, many sisters believe that they are in an all-out fight for their romantic existence.

Victimized by the laws of supply and demand, many very worthy Nubian queens who not many drumbeats ago refused to even consider compromising their standards are now inclined to reassess their traditional position. Now up for serious discussion are controversial issues such as spousal sharing, sisters sponsoring men, and part-time love relationships.

That is why I was particularly concerned when a dear friend of mine, a beautiful chocolate super lady I'll call Candace, called me the other day in anguish about her souring romance.

"Doctor D, I don't know what to do," she said, almost in tears. "This relationship is just not working out. It seems that the more I put in, the less I get out. We seem to have nothing in common anymore."

"So what's the hook?" I calmly asked. "What's keeping you there?"

"I love him," she replied. "I love him so very much."

"What's love got to do with it?" Paraphrasing both Tina and the Bible I said, "Love that doesn't make you happy ain't healthy. You know what I'm saying?" I tried out my best rap imitation on her. She was not impressed.

"For years, he has been the only man in my life. I just can't see myself starting over with someone new."

"Then start over with someone you know, namely *you*," I said. "Get a chance to know yourself. Why do you have this overwhelming compulsion to be with a man? Why is it that some sisters feel like if they have no man they have no life?" I asked.

I might as well have been speaking in Swahili. She completely dismissed my question. "You don't understand. I have six years in this relationship. Six years of my blood, sweat, and tears. That's major time out of my life. Time I can never get back."

"Time is simply speed times distance. If you are going nowhere fast, time loses its meaning," I said, giving her some of my best Ebony Einstein. "I don't understand what time has to do with anything."

I could feel her becoming impatient with my ignorance. "Don't you understand?" she asked. "Six years of my life. *Six whole years.* This relationship has got to work!"

Then, suddenly, a lightning bolt struck me, and I understood. Like Paul on the Damascus road, I saw the light.

"Time," it dawned on me, was the profound variable. Time is the unspoken enigma. The ultimate Truth. A woman's concept of Time is the mystery of mysteries that men don't comprehend. Women see Time differently than men. For men, Time is a function of mechanical physics. It is a measurement of the cycles of the universe. It has no intrinsic value unto itself. It only has value relative to other events in a four dimensional universe.

But for women, Time is different. Time is both a quantity and a quality. It is a process and a value. It has to have a payout, a dividend, like an annuity or a certificate of deposit. Time is capital invested, for which women expect to receive a quantifiable return.

Careful not to come across as cold and insensitive, I politely listened as she sobbed and moaned and justified her position. Needless to say, she made a strong case. I managed to find an opportune moment, induced her to calm down, and shared with her a little story.

"Have you ever read the story of *Moby Dick?*" I asked.

"*Moby Dick?* The book about the Great White Whale?"

"Not quite," I said. "Well, kind of. Actually, it is a story about a man's *obsession* with a great white whale. Moby shows up in the front of the book and in the back of the book, but the real story is about a whaler named Captain Ahab and his fatal attraction to a whale named Moby Dick."

"Go on," said my friend.

"Captain Ahab's claim to fame was that he had never met a whale that he couldn't annihilate—until he met Moby, that is. He had heard that Moby Dick was the biggest, baddest whale in the world, and he couldn't wait until they battled it out. In their tense encounter, Moby snatched Ahab from the boat and bit his leg off. Moby: 1, Ahab: 0. The doctors fitted Ahab with a peg leg, which, for an image-proud old man, was humiliating. That peg leg was a badge of shame, a visible testimony to his humiliating loss to Moby Dick for all the world to see. For years, Ahab fumed. Every time he looked at that leg he burned with hate. Every day he declared that he would one day make Moby Dick pay for taking his leg.

"Finally, Ahab's day came. Commissioned to become the captain on a new whaling boat, he recruited the strongest and best whalers that money could buy. 'Now,' he thought to himself as he looked at his leg, 'It's time for Moby to pay!'

"The ship set sail. For days, the ship journeyed into the deepest part of the water, passing schools of whales along the way. 'Captain,' said the crew, 'afore us are hundreds of the biggest whales that we have ever seen. Why are we passing them?'

"'Because they are not Moby,' retorted Ahab, fuming with the evilness of a hundred demons. He sailed further, cruising past a distressed vessel along the way.

"'Ahab!' shouted the captain of the wounded ship. 'Can you help stranded fellow crewmen?'

"'Have you seen the Great White?' asked Ahab.

"'We saw it go that way,' said the captain.

"'Then I'm going that way,' huffed Ahab, leaving the damaged vessel to fend for itself."

Candace interrupted the story at this point. "That was cold-blooded," she said. I agreed and continued.

"Fueled on by a vociferous volcano of vengeance and vindictiveness, Ahab finally came face-to-face with his old nemesis, Moby Dick. Like a white mountainous iceberg, the giant whale peered at his rival, jettisoning humongous gushes of ocean through its blowhole. The battle was on. The sailors thrust dozens of harpoons into Moby's huge back. Moby took the hits and then charged for more, breaking up pieces of the ship with every charge.

"'You will pay,' howled Ahab, looking at his pathetic wooden leg. 'Hell will freeze over before I'll let you get away with this!' Undaunted, Moby charged again, smashing the boat to pieces.

"'Let him go, Captain!' shouted the crew. 'Let him go before he destroys us all!'

"'I'll never let him go!' screamed Ahab. 'I'll get my revenge. Moby will die if I have to kill him myself.' With that, Ahab jumped overboard, harpoon in hand, and landed on the back of the pale swimming island. 'Die, you wretched beast!' cried Ahab, repeatedly spearing Moby Dick."

"Wow!" said Candace. "What happened next?"

"Well, that was the last time Ahab was ever seen. His crew stood silent, humbled in terror as they watched Moby Dick slowly sink into the abyss with Ahab tied to his back, trapped there by the ropes of the harpoons."

"Goodness!" said my friend.

"Sometimes in life you have to cut your losses," I said. "Moby was not deliberately trying to hurt Ahab, but when a whale wants to be free, it's hard to hold him with a rope."

"What a story!"

"I've got another one for you. Have you ever heard of William Peg Leg Bates?"

"No, who's that?" she asked.

"William Bates was a young Black boy born at the turn of the century. He lived on a farm and he dreamed of being a great tap dancer one day. But when he was a child, he lost his leg in a farming accident."

"How sad," said Candace.

"The doctors fitted him with a wooden leg. He was feeling sorry for himself, felt that his dream of being a great tap dancer was lost forever. That is, until he talked to his mother. His mother, a sharecropper and the daughter of a slave, had seen hard times all of her life. She looked him dead in the eye and said, 'William you are at a crossroad in your life. You can either spend your life moping about the leg you lost, or you can take the one good leg you got left and make something productive out of yourself. Life ain't always fair, but when things don't work out you got to pick up the broken pieces and go on.'"

"William took a deep breath and said, 'Mama, you're right. Just because I lost my leg don't mean that I got to lose my dream.' So William got out one tap shoe, polished his wooden leg, put a tap on it, and taught himself to tap dance on one leg.

"He became a phenomenon, one of the greatest tap dancers on the planet. Calling himself 'Peg Leg Bates,' he became famous all over the world and made a fortune. He appeared on numerous TV shows and stages, and was the first Black to open up a major first-class resort named after himself.

"Unlike Captain Ahab, he took a negative and turned it into a positive. Same ailment, different attitude." I told my friend that she had a choice: she could go through life as Captain Ahab or as Peg Leg Bates.

She could get mired in her circumstances and become obsessed with trying to redeem a bad situation, or she could take a deep breath, cut her losses, rebalance her life on the good leg she was left standing on, and start fresh.

"And in the future," I said before hanging up, "when choosing your mate, think character rather than commerce. Consider depth rather than height. Then put on your new dress, polish up that wooden leg, and take your show on the road. And for goodness' sake, *exhale!*"

Meeting the God Within
Gettye Israel

I vividly recall the traditional summer revival night in the Pine Grove Baptist church. It was filled with the loud sounds of gospel hymns, spirituals, call and response, and fire-and-brimstone preaching. As I watched my peers slowly move toward the preacher and deacons, I nervously found the courage—or pressure—to join the church. That was the night I got my religion.

Later, the baptismal—a big day—arrived. All the recent recruits, dressed in white cloth from head to toe, marched to a nearby man-made lake. We resembled a small army of Christian soldiers—committed and fearless. That all changed when my head was dunked under water; I thought I was drowning. In fact, I fought so hard to come up, the surrounding crowd assumed I was filled with the Holy Spirit and began praising the Lord. I recall thinking afterward that there must be a safer way to serve God.

Religion wasn't that simple for me. In fact, Christianity would prove to be the beginning of a long journey in my search for God.

The future brought about many distinct religious experiences that involved Buddhism, Judaism, Metaphysics, and various Christian denominations. While the belief systems and styles of worship were enlightening, confusing, and interesting, I still did not feel satisfied, compelled, or any closer to the Creator. So, I kept looking and eventually moved up North.

Chicago did not greet me with the warm, hospitable arms that I had grown accustomed to down South. My first year there put me face-to-face with the greatest challenge I have ever faced: homelessness. I found myself in a strange city with no shelter, transportation (thanks to thieves), or job.

Yet, I felt an unbelievable degree of security and protection unlike I had ever felt before. There was an overwhelming sense of something great at work. Furthermore, I knew deep within that this "suffering" was a part of the Creator's divine plan and purpose for me. I also realized that the Creator had not brought me to Chicago to leave me.

I was cut off from my family and other resources. I literally had nowhere to turn. So I turned inward and created this ritual: I turned toward the East and prayed at sunrise and sunset; I read four chapters of the Bible before retiring for the night and upon rising each new day. Every day I exhorted my victory over this tribulation. Although my parents pleaded with me to get on the next Greyhound home, I stayed. I reminded them that I was only experiencing what I had witnessed them endure most of their lives, and that, like them, I had to step out on my faith in the Creator, the same God they had called upon all my life. I chose to see the experience as my test, or as many Christians would say, "my cross to bear." I also chose not to see myself as a victim of society, but a special person undergoing a spiritual cleansing and revolution so as to realize the Creator's purpose for my life. The spirit of the Creator was truly upon me. I never cried or worried, but rested calm and serene in the infinite mind of the Creator. For the first time in my life, I felt strong, fearless, and powerful.

I reflected on the numerous occasions when ministers had exhorted, "Seek ye first the Kingdom of God before all things." I had always been perplexed by that statement, often wondering where and how to look.

Why hadn't they explained that the Kingdom was actually inside of me? With that revelation, I promised the Creator that if He delivered me I would commit my life to his divine purpose.

Surely I was delivered, and in many forms. Technically, I didn't have a "home," but I never spent a night on the streets. I was taken in by eight different men—African, African American, Caucasian, and Hispanic—who looked after me by providing shelter, food, transportation, and brotherly support. *They never ever demanded money or sexual favors in return.*

For thirteen or so years, I had searched for God in the church, mosque, temple, synagogue, the Cross, and yes, even the clouds. In the summer of 1990, I was finally forced to look inside and there I not only found God, but myself. I had come to Chicago in search of God, myself and my life's purpose, and discovered that the Creator was already intricately woven within my being. I had also learned that the Creator is an "infinite living mind"—what most call "spirit"—and that my mind, while finite, was intimately connected.

Today, I am not a part of a religious institution. I choose to simply live each day righteously; to realize and manifest the Creator in every aspect of my life; to acknowledge the universal laws that govern the world; to understand that the answers to my evolution are internal, and that there is no power outside of the Creator that can affect me. And so, when someone asks, "What is your religion?" I pause for a moment and faithfully respond, "The God within."

A Lesson in Consciousness
Haki R. Madhubuti

The education I received in the Black community was entirely different—in content and context—from that of whites. Not only was my "training" not a challenge, it was discouraging. The major piece of information I absorbed after twelve years of public education was that I was a problem, inferior, ineducable, and a victim. And, as a victim, I began to see the world through the eyes of a victim.

I'll never forget how hard my mother worked to make ends meet for my sister and me. Our material lives were impoverished; we didn't have a television, record player, car, telephone, or too much food. We acquired much of our clothing from secondhand stores, and I learned to work the streets very early. My life began to change when I was introduced to other worlds.

One year on my birthday, my mother took me to a five-and-dime store to buy me a gift. She bought me a blue plastic airplane with blue wheels, a blue propeller, and a blue string on the front of the plane so that one could pull it across the floor. I was happy. That following week she took me and my sister to Dearborn, Michigan, where she occasionally did "day work." Day work, for the uninformed, means Black women cleaning up white folks' homes. Dearborn, Michigan, is where many of the movers and shakers who controlled the automobile industry lived. What I quickly noticed was that they lived differently. There were no five-and-dime stores in Dearborn at this time; there were craft shops. This is where the white mothers and fathers bought their children airplanes in boxes. In the boxes were wooden parts, directions for assembly, glue and small engines. Generally, the son would assemble the plane (which might take a day or two) and then take the plane outside and—guess what—it would fly.

This small slice of life is an example of the development—quite early—of two different consciousnesses. In my case and that of other poor youths, we would buy the plane already assembled, take it home and hope it rolled on the floor as if it was a car or truck rather than a plane. In Dearborn, the family would *invest* in a learning toy, and the child would put it together. Through this process, the child would learn work ethics and science and math principles. And, as a result of all that, the plane would *fly*. I was learning to be a consumer who depended on others to build the plane for me. The child in Dearborn made an investment, worked on it and, through his labor and brain power, produced a plane that flew. Translating this to the larger world, I was being taught to buy and to use my body from the neck down, while the white upper-class boy was being taught, very early, to prepare himself to build things and run things, using the neck up. Two different worlds: my world—depending on and working for others, and his world—controlling his own destiny.

Back to the Community
Geoffrey R. Pete

I was born in the all-black community of South Berkeley, California, as was my mother. A loving and supportive woman, she was the epitome of motherhood; family was always first for her. To this day, I cannot remember one school field trip that she missed.

My father moved to Alameda from the South when he was nine years old. He was an interesting man. I guess the psychic memory of all things Southern and then the culture shock of Alameda, which was predominantly white, permanently affected him. On his first day of school, he replied to some question by saying "way over yonder," and the whole class erupted in laughter. Then he said, "out on the galley," which meant the porch, and they laughed again. He said he didn't open his mouth for six months until he spoke impeccable English. Then he quoted from Dunbar and Shakespeare, every chapter and verse.

If my brothers and I ever slipped and said something like, "Where's such and such *at?*" they'd both go off. *"What do you mean 'where's such and such* at'?" My father corrected our English constantly. Now I find myself doing the same thing with my daughter. The assault on language was the ultimate crime of slavery, so speaking in the black vernacular is a surviving Africanism in a sense. It's important to have something that we can claim as our own. The basis for any culture is language and history, that's power. But by the same token, I understand my parents' need to make sure that we were fluent in the "King's English."

I was raised in the church, and that was a very important component of my upbringing and the strength of our community in South Berkeley. Of all the things my parents gave me, church was their greatest gift. One travesty of our present community is that we now have generations that were not raised in the church. As a result, we are struggling with a clash of values that's wreaking havoc with our families and communities.

When I was a young boy, my family moved out of our all-black neighborhood to a predominantly white one. When I moved to the all-white school, I was well equipped for a smooth transition. My fabulous black teachers had prepared me well. Miss Maples loved me and lectured me and snatched me to make sure I took care of business and behaved. Mr. Guest, the janitor, would literally knock sense into our heads. That was great! That was rich! I felt loved at school and at home.

My old black neighborhood in South Berkeley was steeped in black culture. We never knew or understood how rich we were. Sacramento Street, the main thoroughfare in South Berkeley during the 1950s, was legendary. Mr. Rumpford, our first black elected official, had a pharmacy there. Jim McMillan, now a retired city-council person in Richmond, was a young pharmacist. Reids Records was on Sacramento Street, as well as the legendary Lois the Pie Queen. Attorney Tom Berkeley's office was also there. There were insurance brokers and food service companies.

Back then California, like the rest of the country, was segregated, and it was our most powerful time. All the boys were into Little League Baseball, and our parents were actively involved in everything we did. There were as many adults spectating at each game as there were kids. There was never any shortage of playground directors. They were heroic and sheroic figures in the community and ran the parks with an iron fist. There was never a concern about our safety or whereabouts.

One of the travesties of my generation is that we—women and

men—sacrificed family and community for career growth and material wealth. There's something primordial, something inherent in the human experience that we lost. What did we lose? A sense of spirituality, the extended family, compassion. Why did we lose them? We felt the need to minimize our differences with the dominant group, and we severed our ties with community in the process. Michael Jackson represents this tragic personification.

We also lost because black men have abandoned their families *en masse. This is the most critical element of what we lost.* Youngsters today grow up not fearing anyone. Fathers traditionally provided a healthy fear element. I have a recently deceased friend from the South who was a Ph.D./M.D. His father literally screamed at him, "You're going to be a doctor! You're going to be a doctor!" Dr. Carlos Sledge ultimately felt that he would have let his father and community down if he failed. I miss my friend immensely; his sudden death left a void in the hearts of many.

We're on the way back, though, and the defining moment for us was the Million Man March. I took my nephew. Years ago he was shot and is now paralyzed, but he has a good, positive spirit. I felt it was important to take him, and I was right. When Rosa Parks went up on that stage, all million men chanted "Rosa, Rosa, Rosa." It was phenomenal. My nephew was so grateful to be there. Maya Angelou followed and said, "I love one million black men!" Before God, we men humbled ourselves and prayed, "Forgive us, help us." It was the most powerful experience for me, my nephew, and millions of black people. The March showed us what awesome power we have when we come together as one. There were middle-class men, Negroes, militants, professors, fathers and sons, winos (minus the wine), Caribbeans, and Africans. The pigments ranged from light-skinned to pitch black. We all said, "I don't care about perception, I don't care about repercussions, I don't care about the CIA, I don't care about surveillance, I don't care about my government job, I don't care about any of that. Here I stand, on this day, with one aim, one God, one destiny."

The Million Man March was the defining moment of the African American sojourn. Has anything changed since that grand spectacle of black maleness? Yes, and in many ways the changes are immeasurable. We recognized Willie Lynch and others like him as the true authors of slavery, and we announced to the world that we would no longer let hue or hair or status or ideology separate us from our brothers and sisters.

For me, however, the most profound result was that God was brought back into the consciousness of black men. One million black men were saying "God is great," be He Allah, Jehovah, Yaweh, or Elohim. Together we were saying, "I love God, I love my people, I love my race, I love my community."

How the 40oz Can Impair Good Judgement
Alfred "Coach" Powell

Once upon a time in a land called Kamit lived a god-king named Ausar. He was also called Lord of the Perfect Black and the god of fertility. His symbols were the bull, sun, and moon.

Now King Ausar had an evil brother named Seth. Seth was very jealous of Ausar. He hated Ausar so much that he conspired, with 72 other people, to kill him.

Seth and the gang decided to throw a big party, full of wine, women, and song. It was the social event of the season, and King Ausar was the "honored" guest.

Just when the party started to heat up, Seth unveiled a pile of treasures which included, of all things, a casket. Ausar was a rich god-king, but still, the sight of all those treasures excited him. Seth smiled wickedly to his brother and said, "He who can fit his body into the coffin will be rewarded with all these treasures."

His decision making ability severely impaired by the ancient 40oz, King Ausar stumbled into the casket and lay down. Quickly, the ungodly gang sealed the coffin shut with silver molten lead. They threw the coffin into the Nile River and left Ausar to his fate.

Sometime later, Ausar's beautiful sister/wife Isis found the coffin and dragged it out of the Nile. The exercise left her exhausted, so she lay upon it and fell asleep. As fate would have it, Seth just happened to be in the hood, and he was enraged to see that the coffin had been rescued.

By the light of the full moon, Seth took Ausar's body out of the coffin, chopped it up into 14 pieces, and scattered them about the earth. Isis managed to retrieve 13 pieces (she couldn't find the penis). Then she put Ausar back together, prayed for a child, and immaculately (i.e., without sex) conceived a baby boy she named Horus. (By the way, many scholars believe that the story of the immaculate conception of Jesus was taken from the Ausar myth, but that's another story.) Horus eventually grew up to avenge his father's death by killing Seth. And the resurrected Ausar became Lord of the Underworld, Judge of the Dead.

The 42 Principles of Ma'at

Ma'at was the female counterpart to Thoth and was the symbol of truth and justice in the Kemetan worldview. The principles of Ma'at were used as a moral code for the living and the standard that the dead would be judged by. The Kemetans believed that when a person died, his or her soul would be weighed against these principles. Heaven (or hell) would follow.

May the principles of Ma'at guide you in this life and for generations to come.

1. I have not committed sin.

2. I have not committed robbery with violence.

3. I have not stolen.

4. I have not slain men and women.

5. I have not stolen food.

6. I have not swindled offerings.

7. I have not stolen from God.

8. I have not told lies.

9. I have not carried away food.

10. I have not cursed.

11. I have not closed my ears to truth.

12. I have not committed adultery.

13. I have not made anyone cry.

14. I have not felt sorrow without reason.

15. I have not assaulted anyone.

16. I am not deceitful.

17. I have not stolen anyone's land.

18. I have not been an eavesdropper.

19. I have not falsely accused anyone.

20. I have not been angry without reason.

21. I have not seduced anyone's wife.

22. I have not polluted myself.

23. I have not terrorized anyone.

24. I have not disobeyed the law.

25. I have not been excessively angry.

26. I have not cursed God.

27. I have not behaved with violence.

28. I have not caused disruption of peace.

29. I have not acted hastily or without thought.

30. I have not overstepped my boundaries of concern.

31. I have not exaggerated my words when speaking.

32. I have not worked evil.

33. I have not used evil thoughts, words or deeds.

34. I have not polluted the water.

35. I have not spoken angrily or arrogantly.

36. I have not cursed anyone in thought, word or deed.

37. I have not placed myself on a pedestal.

38. I have not stolen that which belongs to God.

39. I have not stolen from or disrespected the deceased.

40. I have not taken food from a child.

41. I have not acted with insolence.

42. I have not destroyed property belonging to God.

What You Think
Is What You Get
Janice C. Hodge

As my patient and I sat in contemplation of the successes and failures in his life, we were stunned at what we learned quite unexpectedly. The wisdom we had been gifted with was not a foreign concept for either of us. Even so, that moment of revelation was a life altering event. Let me provide the history.

Several years ago, a man I'll call Ed began counseling with me. He was deeply depressed at the time and admitted that he had felt so for many years. Still grieving the early death of his mother, struggling to re-cover from childhood sexual abuse, frequent and painful rejection from family and friends and a recurrent health condition, this bright and charming man was most miserable. During one of our early meetings, Ed courageously admitted that the hurt and pain he felt was so extensive that he wished for his death. To ascertain the seriousness of this man's suicidal ideas, I asked, "Do you have a plan for how you would take your life?" Without any hesitation, he poured out his thoughts.

"Sometimes I think that I ought to get into my car and drive down the expressway real fast so that I could crash into something large and nonmoving," he said easily. Those words filled the room with pain and sadness as we both fell silent. Then with laughter he added, "But with

94

my luck, I wouldn't die in that accident, I would just be paralyzed from the neck down."

Grateful for the comic relief, albeit morbid, I laughed with him. My heart, however, felt heavy and my head was swimming in search of the fastest and most effective intervention. I do not recall how we ended our session that day, I only remember my silent prayers for this man as he continued to battle for his life.

Over a period of two years, Ed and I continued to work hard on his concerns. The result was the establishment of a secure relationship that offered a safe place for him to share thoughts and feelings. As time passed, we both rejoiced in the many ways that he had made improvements in his life. He learned new ways to approach relationships with significant others to avoid unnecessary hurt. He improved his personal care, and in turn, his health concerns became more manageable. Overall, the force of continued life crises began to dissipate. The depression that led to the death wish began to lift and there was no more mention of the need to die. Enjoying his enhanced life, Ed decided to discontinue counseling. In my assessment, his decision was premature for while the symptoms of traumatic stress were easing, complete recovery had not yet occurred. In my role of counselor and companion with Ed on his life journey, I advised that it would be best to remain in therapy to circumvent problems that may arise. He still wanted to end his therapeutic work. I did not stand in the way of his decision. Through the years, I often thought about Ed and wondered about how he was doing.

Quite recently, I received a call from Ed. He needed to talk, since he was feeling gravely depressed. When we sat down together once again, Ed spoke quietly and slowly as he released the troubles that tormented his life. A frantic edge shaped his voice tone and quick, jerky movements grasped his body as he told of repeated emotionally abusive relationships and past losses in his life that remained unresolved. Then there was the recounting of a horrible car accident. "Why is this happening to me?" moaned Ed repeatedly. At that moment, an answer emerged within me as I requested that Ed describe the accident.

"I was crossing the street one winter evening. Suddenly, this car appeared out of nowhere. It was moving real fast and I couldn't clear the street in enough time to avoid the collision. The next thing I remember is arriving at the hospital by ambulance. One arm and both of my legs were broken. I had to go into rehabilitation to learn how to walk again. I couldn't work. For months, I was totally helpless. Why does God let these things happen to me?" he asked weakly.

After some of Ed's anguish quieted, I carefully asked him if he remembered a conversation we had had several years ago. He waited to hear what I had to say. I recounted the words he declared in expressing his heartfelt desire to die by a planned car accident. I repeated to him what he supposed would be a probable outcome of such an accident. The catastrophic vision that Ed had spoken about had occurred the way he spoke of it. As this realization penetrated us both, we sat in pregnant silence meditating on the meaning of the situation. Gently, I said, "Well, Ed, now that you see the power you have to bring destruction into your life by harboring threatening thoughts and speaking damaging words, how much more is the opposite true. You can also bring pleasure and satisfaction to yourself by harboring excellent thoughts and by speaking of what is healthy and beneficial for your life. You have the power within yourself to transform your life."

Only time will tell how much the revelation we experienced that day will impact Ed's life. As for me, I experienced immediate growth and change as I reconsidered unhelpful attitudes that I have maintained in my own life. Even as I examined some of the vexing problems that concern most of us in our community, that sudden encounter with ancient wisdom was liberating. My mind turned to one of my favorite historical models, Maria Stewart. She was a strong person who likely was the first Black woman to make a public effort on behalf of the advancement of her people in America. During a time when Blacks were viewed as subhuman, Maria refused to see herself or her people that way. She recognized the power we hold within us to transform our lives and the world around us. Noting despair, depression, and stagnation among her people in the early 1800s, she reminded them that skin color does not make the person but, rather, the principles that are formed within the soul. "Do not let your hearts be any longer discouraged; it is no use to murmur or repine; but let us promote ourselves and improve our own talents. 'I can't' is a great barrier in the way. I hope it will soon be removed, and 'I will' resume its place."[1]

Take these next moments and consider your current thoughts and feelings. Do you ever say, "I can't"? What negative thoughts have you hidden in your heart and mind? Do you feel there is no hope for you? Listen to the conversations you have with yourself and others. Be gently truthful with your self-examination. Erase the "I can't" and the "I will never be able to" from your inner thoughts. Search out and replace the damaging beliefs about yourself that you may have gathered from family, friends, and society. Uproot any toxic thoughts and plant loving and nurturing concepts of yourself. This is not an easy task, but it is greatly worth the effort.

Seek out the support of trustworthy and positive people. Discover books to read that promote healthy life perspectives. Involve yourself in strong and affirming churches, groups, and organizations. If you need to, don't be ashamed to talk to a caring and well-trained professional who remains committed to her or his own personal growth. As one pastor says, "You cannot soar with the eagles if you are running with the turkeys."

The experience that I shared with Ed prompted new attitudes in my own life by reinforcing my faith in myself, my history and traditions, my family and friendships, and my hope for the African American community. Above all, I experienced reassurance in my relationship with God. I pray your faith becomes strengthened and leads you to accomplish and receive all that your heart desires.

[1] *Black Women in Nineteenth Century Life. Pgs.* 183–88; *Lowenberg and Bogin, 1981.*

How to Search for Truth
George Washington Carver

> More and more as we come closer and closer in touch
> with nature and its teachings are we able to see the Di‐
> vine and are therefore fitted to interpret correctly
> the various languages spoken by all forms of nature
> about us.
> —*George Washington Carver, 24 February 1930*

I believe the Great Creator of the universe had young people in mind
when the following beautiful passages were written:

In the 12th chapter of Job and the 7th & 8th verses, we are urged
thus: But ask now the beasts and they shall teach thee; and the fowls of
the air, and they shall tell thee.

Or speak to the earth, and it shall teach thee; and the fishes of the sea
shall declare unto thee.

In St. John the 8th chapter and 32nd verse, we have this remarkable
statement: And ye shall know the truth and the truth shall make you free.

Were I permitted to paraphrase it, I would put it thus: And you shall
know science and science shall set you free, because science is truth.

There is nothing more assuring, more inspiring, or more literally true than the above passages from Holy Writ.

We get closer to God as we get more intimately and understandingly acquainted with the things he has created. I know of nothing more inspiring than that of making discoveries for ones self.

The study of nature is not only entertaining, but instructive and the only true method that leads up to the development of a creative mind and a clear understanding of the great natural principles which surround every branch of business in which we may engage. Aside from this it encourages investigation, stimulates and develops originality in a way that helps the student to find himself more quickly and accurately than any plan yet worked out.

The singing birds, the buzzing bees, the opening flower, and the budding trees, along with other forms of animate and inanimate matter, all have their marvelous creation story to tell each searcher for truth. . . .

We doubt if there is a normal boy or girl in all Christendom endowed with the five senses who has not watched with increased interest and profit, the various forms, movements and the gorgeous paintings of the butterfly, many do not know, but will study with increased enthusiasm the striking analogy its life to the human soul.

Even the ancient Greeks with their imperfect knowledge of insects recognized this truth, when they gave the same Greek name psyche to the soul, or the spirit of life, and alike to the butterfly.

They sculptured over the effigy of their dead the figure of a butterfly floating away as it were in his breath. Poets to this day follow the simile.

More and more as we come closer and closer in touch with nature and its teachings are we able to see the divine and are therefore fitted to interpret correctly the various languages spoken by all forms of nature about us.

From the frail little mushroom, which seems to spring up in a night and perish ere the morning sun sinks to rest in the western horizon, to the giant redwoods of the Pacific slope that have stood the storms for centuries and vie with the snow-capped peaks of the loftiest mountains, in their magnificence and grandeur.

First, to me, my dear young friends, nature in its varied forms are the little windows through which God permits me to commune with Him, and to see much of His glory, majesty, and power by simply lifting the curtain and looking in.

Second, I love to think of nature as unlimited broadcasting stations, through which God speaks to us every day, every hour and every moment of our lives, if we will only tune in and remain so.

Third, I am more and more convinced, as I search for truth, that no ardent student of nature can "Behold the lilies of the field"; or "look until the hills," or study even the microscopic wonders of a stagnant pool of water, and honestly declare himself to be an infidel.

To those who already love nature, I need only to say, pursue its truths with a new zest, and give to the world the value of the answers to the many questions you have asked the greatest of all teachers—

Mother Nature.

To those who have as yet not learned the secret of true happiness, which is the joy of coming into the closest relationship with the Maker and Preserver of all things: begin now to study the little things in your own dooryard, going from the known to the nearest related unknown, for indeed each new truth brings one nearer to God.

With love and best wishes,

G. W. CARVER

The Bus Ride Home
Jauqo Kelly

For many years I thought that the way in which I was living was the only way to live. Crime was my religion. I breathed it, ate it, and simply lived for it. In my heart I always wanted there to be more to life than the choices I had made, but I was addicted. Doing crime was a definite high. I loved the excitement of almost getting caught, then getting away with the crime. Perhaps, deep within, I wanted to get caught.

I had no social ties other than to the small circle of individuals with whom I was committing crimes. We would sit around and contemplate what crimes to commit and how to implement them. While planning my crimes, I always carried the thought that no matter how well I calculated, one day I would be caught. A criminal who is in tune with his "spiritual" criminality knows that one day he will slip. Spiritual criminality simply means that I was consumed by crime. Crime was my god, my idol, my life impetus, and nothing else mattered outside of that. My devotion to crime was no different from that of devout Christians who live and breathe the Bible.

When I finally graduated to the penitentiary, I took that inevitable bus ride down South. All I could think was, "I finally made it." I looked around and 98 percent of the inmates were men of color, mostly African

American. While in prison I plotted and schemed my return to crime upon my release. It was impossible to automatically turn off that mindset. If that way of thinking is all a man knows, he will remain addicted to it. Only a spiritual awakening can save him.

One day when I was lying in my cell, I had an out-of-body experience. I actually saw my body, or what appeared to be my body, step outside of itself and turn toward me. I saw myself ask me, "What the f— are you going to do when you get out of the joint?" That experience was the turning point in my life when my thoughts began to change. I looked at my life and realized I was getting old. I saw other inmates who had been incarcerated twenty, thirty, forty years—longer than I had been on earth—and they were never getting out. I decided that I did not want to be in jail forever and made a commitment never to return.

I began to think about my talents, which were acting and playing music. I thought that I'd like to try and pursue a career in which I could make active use of my talents.

I was in prison for six years, and was finally released in 1992. Since gaining my freedom, I have taken advantage of the opportunities to do very simple things that I had taken for granted before being imprisoned, such as going to a wedding and to the city zoo, which I had last visited when I was in grade school.

During this transformation, I began cutting certain people loose— friends and associates who had grown into this life of crime with me. There was often conflict, because they associated my desire to change with weakness. However, they often ended up back in prison, sometimes even for life.

The temptation to commit crime has definitely been there, and so I see myself as a recovering addict, no different from a drug user or alcoholic. What helps me stay focused, however, are my bass guitar, which I've been playing for twenty years (even played while I was in prison) and the development of my other talents.

The two bus rides to and from prison played a crucial role in my transformation. During the bus ride to prison my thoughts were, "I'm going to a place I've never been before. I don't know if I'll come out alive." On the bus ride from prison I thought, "I'm going to a new world, one that I've been in before; however, it's new because this is where the test starts." The test actually started when I boarded that bus and headed for home. I was more terrified about going home than about going to prison.

I knew that my prayers and promises about wanting to play music professionally and contributing something positive to the community, especially for my daughter, were about to be tested. I would have to prove that I was sincere about wanting to change, even in the midst of poverty, crime, and former friends flashing wads of money.

Overall, I've learned that a man will get out of prison what he wants out of it. I know for a fact that there is no program of rehabilitation in the penal system—not as Americans would like to believe. The only way an inmate will become rehabilitated is if he or she decides to use that time to study, heal, and grow. This will happen only if change is truly desired. We, especially Black men, cannot continue down the path that we're currently traveling. If I had allowed it, this type of mentality eventually would have destroyed me spiritually, mentally, and physically. I can never allow myself to forget either, because if I forget my prison experience, there is a great probability that I will return.

Today, I have a nine-member band called Mystical Entity. The music we play is very spiritual, and it touches not only the hearts of people of color but also many whites. I've also discovered that there are some white people who have the essence of Africa flowing through their beings and that one doesn't need to be Black to appreciate the spiritual struggle between good and evil.

As I move through my transformation, I continue to nurture my dearest relationship with my mother, daughters, siblings, and a few progressive friends. They reaffirm my new purpose and new existence. I now have a healthy, life-giving and receiving spirit. Furthermore, I am truly committed to living up to my responsibilities as a man, father, son, and member of the African American community. I just hope and pray that the music I play is a testimony to all of this.

A Mother's Reaffirming Love
Ron Mitchell

As I've grown and matured, my relationship with my mother has blossomed, but it wasn't always so good. When I was a boy, my mother hated men. Now I understand why, but while I was growing up, life under her roof was difficult.

We grew up very poor, and my mother, a single parent, struggled at a low-paying job, trying to make ends meet. All of my mother's children had different fathers. When I was a boy, she would always speak fatalistically about men. She'd say that men were no good and would mess up a good woman. Her words, along with the bad male role models in my neighborhood—the pimps, pushers, and drug dealers who manipulated women to get anything they desired—instilled the idea within my subconscious that men really were bad.

Seeing the influence that men often had on women, I began to accept that perhaps my mother was right. Listening to the only woman in my life, whom I admired and loved so much, denounce all men, and then looking at myself and realizing that I was a male, hurt me more than either of us could have imagined.

She had always told me that I would never be anything, that I would never amount to anything, and that I was like every other man. She used the word "nigger" a lot.

I decided I would prove her wrong. I vowed to treat women the way I wanted my mother to be treated. I imagined that if someone were to look up the word "man" in the dictionary, there would be a picture of me smiling. That's what I wanted; however, despite my best intentions, the psychological damage had been done.

When I became a young man, I dated tons of women. I couldn't settle down with one woman because of lust and a lack of discipline. In the back of my mind, I could hear my mother's voice saying, "You're just like the rest of them." Just as she had predicted, I exploited the hearts and souls of women, just as she had been exploited by the men in her life. Yet the commitment I had made to myself when I was a boy still weighed heavily on my heart. I simply had not sought the courage and catalyst to change.

The final phase of my search for manhood occurred while I was in college. As usual, I was dating a number of women. There was one young woman I really liked a lot. I was very supportive of her, but not faithful to her.

One night while we were in my dorm room, she and I had a big argument. I found out that she had been intimate with one of my friends. I couldn't understand how she could cheat on me because, in my own unhealthy way, I thought I had been good to her. Even though I had done bad things to so many women, I could not handle her infidelity. I was overcome with feelings of rage, anger, betrayal, and of course, self-absorption.

I passed out and suffered a nervous breakdown. I woke up in a hospital, tubes coming out of various parts of my body. I could not move any part of my body, nor could I feel anything except my heart beating. I could also hear voices in my head, particularly that of my mother's saying, "It's over. You can't continue what you've been doing because it has come

back to haunt you. Be a man and take responsibility for your actions."
Then I heard God saying, "You have to change. This is your final opportunity. You can either move forward or backward."

Soon after I left the hospital, my life did begin to change for the better, although slowly. My past behavior was replaced with prayer, meditation, and the Bible—all of which brought me closer to God. I asked
God to help me to not be promiscuous. I realized that in order to achieve
discipline, I would not only need faith in God, but I would truly need to
love myself. For the first time in my life, I asked myself, "Ron, do you really love yourself?" Around the same time we were all shocked and sad-
dened by Magic Johnson's revelation that he was HIV positive. When I
heard the news I prayed, "God, what are you trying to tell me? Will this
happen to me too if I don't change my ways?" I knew that if it could happen to Magic, it could certainly happen to me. Undoubtedly, this was the
final catalyst I needed for maturity.

From that point on, I began to look at all women differently. Soon
thereafter, the woman I needed and wanted to please most phoned me. "I
love you," she said softly and without reservation. For the first time in my
life, my mother, the woman who brought me into the world, reaffirmed
my value and manhood. The first gift my mother gave me was my life.
Those three simple, but powerful, words are the second most significant
gift she has ever given me.

Lessons Learned from Failure
James L. Lasenby

I've always felt an intense sense of responsibility for Black people, my people. Ultimately, I've always wanted my service to manifest in the creation of global commerce among people of African descent. So, I decided the best way to accomplish this was through law school.

I pursued my legal education at Chicago Kent Law School, a highly challenging endeavor, both financially and intellectually. This period was the hardest phase of my life. I did a lot of crying because every aspect of my life was very stressful. I was heavily burdened in school by an enormous load of classes and bills. In addition, my significant relationships were failing. Somehow, however, I developed stamina and a strong will. Going to law school was like running a marathon; graduation was crossing the finish line.

Almost, that is. I still had to take the bar exam, which was extremely difficult. I failed it the first time I took it. This was my first experience of failure—a heavy psychological trip that left me deeply depressed.

Eventually, I pulled myself together, dusted myself off, and immediately stepped back into the ring. Unlike most of my peers, I didn't take time off to rest or relax, and I'm glad I didn't. I passed the exam the second time around. This was a major victory, because failing it had been the most immediate obstacle to my success.

Today, I have an office in the Merchandise Mart, an upscale address in downtown Chicago. I am practicing fifty percent of my time in international business just as I had planned. Primarily, my plan is to exclusively and totally fund, structure, and finance business deals for Black folks in America who are doing business with Black people throughout the diaspora, particularly Africa.

I strongly believe that this is the only way that Africans throughout the world can develop a true economy. If I don't do it, then someone will, so why not me? I feel a great sense of responsibility knowing that I'm not just working hard for myself but for the uplift of Black people in general. I further believe that each of us is born with a divine purpose, something that far exceeds our materialistic and individualistic goals. We are to use our gifts in service to humankind, particularly those of our own racial group.

Essentially, one must have a true vision and be passionate about it. If I stay true to my vision, I know it will develop into what I desire and need it to be. It's a commitment I've made to myself, and, most importantly, to my people.

Lessons on the Playground of Life

Michelle R. Dunlap

Recently, my beautiful brown eight-year-old nephew was playing on a playground as I was taking care of some work-related business in an establishment nearby. Within minutes, he came inside to find me. He looked very sad and began to explain that something had happened on the playground. I thought that maybe he and another child couldn't agree on who would swing first or who would slide next or something like that. But the situation that was bothering him was very different, much more profound.

I stopped what I was doing, looked into his eyes, and asked him to tell me what was wrong. He explained that as he was approaching the playground, he noticed two women talking. When one of the women took notice of my nephew, she looked at her watch and said to the other woman, "Oh my, look at the time!" She then hurriedly grabbed her children, or as my nephew says, "she just *ran away* with the children!" I asked him what exactly bothered him about her leaving with her children—perhaps she really was in a hurry. He said he just had a feeling that it had something to do with him because of the way that she was staring at him when she grabbed her children. And then my eight-year-old nephew just came right out and told me, "I think that she took them away because I am Black."

Inside, my heart was racing as I watched my baby struggling with this whole concept. A thousand thoughts flooded my mind: "Is he old enough to pick up on these things? Maybe she really was in a hurry. But he's a smart kid, and it's not like he's an alarmist—he's never said this kind of thing before. How was he behaving out on the playground when this happened? Who were these people? I'd like to find them and get to the bottom of this!"

I composed myself and calmly asked him if the people were still out there. "No," he said. I asked him if he had been on his very best behavior. "Yes!"

First, validate his experience, I thought to myself. So I said to him, "Robert, you are a smart child, and you know when something is not right. You know when something is up." I then invited him to come and walk with me onto the playground. Once out there, I asked him to pick his favorite spot on the playground. He picked the top of this huge wooden block contraption. It was painted yellow and blue and red. We sat on the very top of it.

What do I want to tell him? I asked myself. Again, a thousand thoughts came flooding as my heart pounded. *I want him to know that it's not his fault and that he has every right to be on this playground and that it was not because of anything that he had done that caused the people to behave the way that they did. I don't want him to blame himself. I don't want him to think that he is bad inside or that something is wrong with him.* There was so much that I wanted to tell him that I really didn't know where to begin. I just got quiet and prayed inside and began to find the words. This is what I said to him:

"Robert, I want you to look at me. Look into my eyes and try to trust everything that I am about to tell you. I am about to explain some things that may be difficult for you to fully understand right now, but you are just going to have to trust me.

"The first thing that I want you to know is that this is not your fault. You have done *nothing* wrong. You were just coming out to play on the playground just like any other child would want to do. If anyone had any problems with that, then it is their problem and their sickness. Not yours.

"The second thing that I want you to know is that what you experienced today is nothing new. Your uncles have experienced it as well as your grandfather, his father, and his father. Many African American people experience this. I have experienced it also. It comes from something that began hundreds and hundreds of years ago by some evil, greedy people. It did not just start today. It was very sick back then, and it is still sick today. It comes from some people trying to make themselves believe that they are better than other people.

"Not everyone is like this. But some people just haven't let go of the prejudice sickness. This is *their* problem. Do not let it rub off on you. You are good, you are beautiful and as perfect as God wanted you to be. Your face is handsome and your smile is beautiful. Your skin and your rich color are beautiful. Your hands and legs and toes and everything that God gave you are beautiful. Your mind is sharp and full of excellent ideas. You are special and brilliant and precious, just like we all are in our own individual ways.

"Don't let that negative energy change what's inside of you. It's okay to say 'I'm hurt,' and if you want to cry about it or shout about it, that's okay. I'm here to help you through that. But don't give up the beautiful spirit that is inside of you because of someone else's ignorance. Let people like that woman live in her blindness, but don't you change who you are. You have done nothing wrong, my dear child. You must trust me, *you have done nothing wrong!*"

For the rest of the afternoon, he tightly held my hand as we went about our errands. He just held onto me, and I held onto him. I rubbed his little face and reminded him to keep his head up high, and he beamed from the support. The incident brought us closer together while further preparing both of us for the many daily micro-aggressions that he may experience as a young African American male in this society. This was a painful, yet valuable, experience for this child. Just one fleeting moment on the playground of life.

In My Image

James Williams

I was raised in a Christian home that taught me not to have a child until I married. Ironically, at twenty years of age, I found myself fathering a son, James Williams, Jr. Based upon my rearing and spiritual beliefs, that was a very difficult thing for me to accept. So the decision I made was to go out, become successful, then take care of my son.

Deep down, however, I saw my son's conception as God's punishment. What had I done to deserve this burden? I had my flaws like everybody else, but I wasn't a bad man. I felt victimized by his mother. She trapped me. Needless to say, my attitude about fatherhood was unhealthy.

My acceptance of my son came about when I was studying in Togo, Africa. I recall asking God to help me accept my son. I did not ask how or why, but simply to be blessed to accept him. I also asked that my son accept me. Slowly but surely I began to change. That metamorphosis occurred as a result of watching African men who were often my age or younger—certainly poorer. I saw them consistently embracing their responsibilities as men and fathers. From African men I learned that being a father was a *blessing*, not a burden.

Soon after I came back to the States, I had my first test of being a father. One chilly day my son and I went to the movie theater to see *Teenage Mutant Ninja Turtles*. While waiting for the show to begin, we decided to window shop. We entered a Warner Brothers store that sells memorabilia from popular movies. I had about $120 on me. The store was especially cool. I asked him why he wasn't wearing a jacket. At that point, it dawned on me that it was cold out and my son needed a jacket. I became determined not to leave that store without getting him a jacket. So, I directed him to go and pick out a jacket. There were approximately thirty jackets in the store to choose from. The prices ranged from $10 to $100. Needless to say, he selected the $100 Batman jacket. I realized that it meant more for me to buy a jacket that he really liked rather than one just to keep him warm. Ironically, he had also picked out a jacket that I would have wanted. I had no qualms or hesitations about paying for the jacket; I just did it. That's when I knew that he was my son and I was his father.

Having James, Jr. in my life has made me realize that I can no longer let just anyone in my life. I've become more selective with the women I date. I now prefer an exclusive relationship with a woman or nothing at all. I'm only interested in being with someone I truly care about, perhaps someone I've known for a while. There used to be a time when I didn't care if everyone was sleeping around. Now I do.

When you become the authority figure in a child's life, you become more aware of how you should be living. My son has caused me to be more conscious. One day we were driving in my car and he said, "I want to be like you, Dad." I don't know why, but he thinks I'm cool. On another day, we were together and we were both wearing suits. He had just gotten a haircut and was brushing his hair when he said, "I want my hair to be wavy like yours." I said, "James, that's not important," but he said, "But I want to be just like you." I realized then that this young man is watching every move I make, and whether my moves are good or bad, he's going to interpret them as good. So it has become more important than ever that my behavior and attitudes are correct.

Once I chaperoned a field trip for his class. While we were on the school bus, his classmates asked him, "James, is that your father?" I was probably the youngest father ever to show up at the school. I'm thirty-one, James is eleven, and all the other parents are between forty and fifty years old. Nevertheless, I felt very good because I had done something for him—at my own expense. I had informed my employer that I was not coming in because I would be spending the day with my son. It just felt good to do that, and the fact that he asked me made me feel very special.

Overall, my son has caused me to be very responsible. I feel now that there is a different reason for my success, and that is my desire for his success. In fact, I want him to be more successful than me—not necessarily in terms of material possessions, but I want him to learn how to make good decisions. If I can get him to learn from my mistakes, his will truly be enough for me.

When my son gets to high school, he's going to need me more than ever before. As he's thinking and shaping ideas, I need to be there to say, "Talk to me more; let me know what you are feeling and thinking." I don't have all the answers, but I do have past experiences and some wisdom that he can draw on. For instance, if he says, "Dad, I want to join a gang," I don't have to get pissed about it because half of my family are gang members, and I used to gang-bang. So there is no need for me to get upset and call on God in a spirit of panic. I can help him through it, give him some strategies.

By the same token, he may come to me and express an interest in being a banker. Well, I can talk about that too because I was once a banker. If he's having problems in school, I can tell him what not to say to his professor.

I also have a cool relationship with his mom (who is beautiful and very smart), thanks to her. Anyone else would have shot me and hung me out to dry and would have been perfectly justified in doing so. That's how much of an ass I was during the early days. She was very calm and patient with me. Without a doubt, I submit that the success of my son will come about because of the parenting partnership that she and I share.

Overall, I compare my relationship with my son to that of mine with God. God made me in His image and while I do not profess to be God, I do strive to implement God-like qualities in my life for my own and, most importantly, my son's sake.

STEP THREE

Soaking the Peas

"We're going to do what I call a 'quick soak,'" said Daddy once I had finished sorting the peas to his satisfaction.

"Why do you have to soak them at all? Why can't you just cook them?" I asked. He took one of the peas out of the bowl and handed it to me.

"Feel it. Squeeze it." I did.

"So?"

"Feel how hard that little thing is?" I nodded. "Want that rock in your stomach like that? Want some really bad gas?" I frowned. "The only thing that'll soften that pea up is a lot of soaking."

"But you said we're going to do a quick soak."

"Right, 'cause we ain't got all day. You're really supposed to leave them soaking overnight, but a quick soak'll have to do." Daddy retrieved an old stewing pot that wobbled when he put it on the stove. "Fill this pot with water—"

"How many cups?" I asked.

Exasperated, he said, "Just fill it about three-quarters of the way up." I looked at him doubtfully. "Gone!" he said. I did as he said, then laid the pot on the stove.

"Now what?" I asked.

"Put the peas in the pot, and turn the heat on high. We're gonna let it boil two minutes—"

"Two? That quick?"

"Two minutes to boil, one hour to soak."

"Oh," I said. "Quick soak." He nodded. I turned on the flame and before long, the bubbles formed and foam from the peas was rising to the top. After two minutes of bubbling and boiling, I turned off the stove.

"Now what?" I asked, setting the timer for one hour. My father handed me some carrots, onions, and celery.

"Here, chop these up," he said, closing his eyes and snapping his fingers to "The A Train." Now that he had tuned me out, I could relax again. I got to chopping. But that hardly took any time at all. After a few minutes, I was done.

"Hey, Daddy! What should I do now?" I asked.

He snapped his fingers and hummed a few bars.

"Oh, Daddy?" He opened one eye and squinted at me. "What do I do now?"

He closed his eye and started snapping his fingers. "You wait."

Our heroine is anxious to start cooking, but her father tells her to have patience. As a single working mother, she's often short on patience. Once she peeks inside the pot to check on the progress of the soaking peas, but her father shoos her away. Patience. Add to that a big helping of persistence and endurance—not a bad recipe for life, she thinks, as she paces the kitchen floor.

Crowning Glory
Kecia Lynn

I want to cut my hair, and I want to do it right now. Movie scenes come to me: Natalie Wood in *Splendor in the Grass*, pruning her hair like a bush; Faye Dunaway as Joan Crawford going at her daughter's flaxen curls in *Mommie Dearest*. The beat of the bass in the club where I work keeps time with the swelling, dramatic soundtrack in my head.

It's been the hottest summer anyone can recall; the entire month of June was 90 degrees and up, and July isn't getting any better. Everywhere I go I see women with bare, cool napes and short, short hair. All the long-haired women I see look uncomfortable no matter how many barrettes and bobby pins they use. They sit and sigh and lift their hair away from their necks, as if gravity won't act sooner or later.

I'm in the ladies' restroom looking at the ends of my hair. They are dry, broomlike. I could paint a canvas with them. Some of my customers are fussing at the mirror. Sisters, for the most part. They are brilliant, perspiring, putting on lipstick, and combing their hair with neon-colored, dagger-toothed utensils. Spritzing and powdering for the men who wait outside. I wash my hands with cold water, try not to look at myself in the mirror.

"Nice hair," one of the sisters says to me, stroking my ponytail and startling me into looking up. She smiles, dark, purple silk dress, blue eye-shadow.

"Gorgeous," another one says, lighter, brown suit, beige lace bustier. "Just let me get mine half as long as that. Is it natural?"

"Got to be," the purple silk woman says. "Can't fake color like this."

"Are you a hairdresser?" I ask.

"Yes," she says.

"I want to get it cut," I blurt. "Can you do it now?"

It was as if I'd announced that I was a lesbian. Twelve women pause in their primping and stare at me.

"Why would you want to cut that hair?" someone says.

There is a chorus of agreement. "*Yeah. For real. I'm saying. O-kay?*"

"Do you want a trim?" the purple silk hairdresser asks me.

"No, I want it cut," I say. I know I sound like I'm making an appeal. "If you had hair like this—"

"I'd put it up in a bun," says the beige lace woman. Her hair is chin-length and cinnamon-colored. She has gold coins for eyes.

"Have you ever worn your hair short?" the hairdresser asks me.

"No," I say.

"What do you think your man would say?"

From the back someone cries, "Girl, if you want to cut it, cut it. It's your hair. The man ain't gotta take care of it. You do."

The hairdresser gently removes my black scarf and fluffs my hair out around me. I look in the mirror for the woman who spoke. All I see are wide eyes, rimmed with color. "I can't believe you want to cut that," someone else says.

"It's so hot," I say, looking down at the sinks, trying to explain. "It's so heavy. I feel like I'm being weighed down. I can hardly move." I'm murmuring now, talking to myself. I can feel my hair hugging me like a fat relative.

"Why don't you look at yourself?" the hairdresser says. She has a round face, and her hair is a shining black cap. "Don't look at me, girl, look at yourself."

I look at myself. I have a thin, sallow face. I have freckles and large brown eyes like my mother. I have too much hair like my mother. I see her sitting at her vanity, lifting her hair from her neck and back with two hands, flapping it to create a breeze, sighing. "Your mother has beautiful hair," my father says. "All woman should have hair like that. Hair is a woman's crowning glory." My mother releases her hair and it tumbles down her back, off the stool, almost to the carpet, curling just at the ends, as an afterthought. My hair was always curlier than hers, compliments of my father. It's no one color. Most of it's brown, some of it's red, some dark blonde. It spreads behind and around and down me like a superhero's cape.

I grab my hair with my hands, clutch it back, tie it with the scarf. I turn and look at the women. Some of them shrug. One white woman says, "What's the big deal? It'll always grow back."

The sisters roll their eyes at her, at each other.

I go back to the bar. "Harry," I say, "where can I find some scissors?"

"In the office, maybe. Hey," his heavy dark hand clamps onto my shoulder, "where you think you going? What you need scissors for? We got customers here."

When I was seven, some of the girls in my neighborhood tried to cut off my hair. They pinned me down behind our garage and threatened me with scissors. The ground was hot, it was summer, the scissors were long and blindingly silver. Stuck-up yellow bitch, they said, caressing my hair with their eyes. They had cut off part of my left ponytail before my father showed up yelling and waving his arms. At first he wouldn't let my mother cut off the remaining hair. She had to show him, by unbraiding and combing, what I would look like with lopsided hair. Even then he said, "She can wear it back, right?" My mother ended up cutting the rest of my hair to even it out. It was the first and only time she'd ever defied him when it came to my hair.

He called the girls' parents and demanded that they be punished for what they did. He didn't speak to my mother for several days. He kept me inside for most of that summer. I sat at the window in my bedroom, reading. When I wasn't reading I was staring at the girls who hated me as they tore up and down the street on bicycles, shouting and laughing at each other. I stared at them and thought about cutting off both ponytails at their roots, throwing them away, burning them.

But then my father would look at me, so sad, as if he'd lost something. I never wanted him to be sad. And it was so easy for us, he would say, hugging me. Our hair made us unique. Us, me and my mother, his women.

At eleven, the purple silk hairdresser hands me her card. It says MARION MORSE. "I have an opening tomorrow at three," she says. "But you'd better call early to get it. The shop opens at nine." She smiles a warm plum-lipsticky smile and walks away.

Sixteen hours from now. I try to visualize the scissors in the back office, lying in a drawer like Arthur's Excalibur. I see myself going into the office, picking up the scissors, putting them to my hair, making that first, greedy bite. It would be too much hair for the scissors to handle. They would not be sharp enough. I would try again. They would chew at it. It would take all night.

There's a guest DJ working tonight. He is younger than me, and he has a posse of three, including a woman with a bad weave. It's the woman who comes up for drinks for the DJ and his friends. She would be pretty if it weren't for the knots of hair tied clumsily to her head.

"Don't get uppity," my mother said the day after the incident. "That's why those girls tried to cut off your hair. 'Cause you were acting uppity."

"No I wasn't, Mama."

"Don't talk back to me! They all want what we got. 'Cause they know that's what looks good. They don't know how to do for themselves, so they gotta do what they can. Don't think you any better than them, though, 'cause you're not."

If that's true, Mama, then how come you wouldn't let me cut my hair? How come you never let me cut my hair?

"Course, if it was up to me, you'd been had your hair cut," she said. Muttered, rather, under her breath, so I wouldn't hear.

At 2:30, I go into the office. My bosses, the couple who own the club, turn from the desk and look at me as if I were a criminal. "Do you have any scissors?" I ask, expecting them to say no. But Mr. Jefferson reaches into the desk drawer and pulls out a pair and gives it to me. They are not the long gleaming scissors I imagined at the bar. The handles are orange plastic, the blades brushed silver. I put my fingers in the handles, and the blades open and close with a clean, complete sound. STAINLESS, one of the blades reads.

"Anything else?" Mrs. Jefferson snaps.

I rush out and down to the ladies' restroom. The bar is closed, but the music still plays, so there are still customers fussing and painting. There is one woman in line for a toilet. I stand behind her, clutching the scissors. I see myself in the mirror across from the row of toilets. My face is shiny, with little wisps of hair clinging, trying to creep forward. The scissors resemble a silver-and-orange crucifix pressed to my chest.

In the stall, I gather my hair up at the back of my head and tie it tightly with the black scarf. I hold onto the ponytail with one hand and cut in front of the scarf with the other. I feel the ponytail disengaging it-self from my head, bit by bit. The scissors move faster and the music picks up with it, drumming heavy and hard. Then there is a loud snap as the blades come together and my hair falls in a lump from my head. Air rushes to my head, ballooning it. There is nothing at my nape. There is nothing holding my head to the earth. I stare at the ponytail in my lap from high up. It looks like a dead animal, a stole to wrap around someone's neck. Untidy, unthreatening. I force my fingers through what's left, raking my scalp with my nails to spread it out a bit. Then I touch my long neck, my shoulders, my bare arms, my breath coming out of me in one great, heavy sigh.

I open the door to my parents' house slowly. In the living room the long, low cocktail table has a dish of salted peanuts on it. I take my ponytail out of my bag and lay it on the table. The white scarf I've used to tie together its other end flashes blue with the streetlight coming through the picture window.

As I tiptoe to my room I can hear them snoring in counterpoint. My hands are drawn again to my loose, helium head. The hair there has been straightened by years of weight, but it will curl up when it's washed. The ends are sharp and new against my fingertips. In six hours I will call Marion Morse and make an appointment to have her help me finish the job.

Shake It Up!

Stephanie J. Gates

The words "belly dancing" leaped off the page of the Harold Washington College Continuing Education Catalog. Looking for something to do one summer I thought, Here's my chance to fulfill my secret desire to be an exotic dancer of some sort.

Since I had seen belly dancers only on TV or in the movies, my perception of the dance had been shaped by the media. So, you can imagine my surprise when, instead of a mythical, voluptuous Middle Eastern woman, my instructor turned out to be tall, slim, and Black.

Though I had only the vaguest notion of what belly dancing was, I thought it would be a fun, easy class. Wrong! The most difficult techniques for me to master were the "overrolls" and "underrolls." Standing straight with the knees slightly bent, we had to push our hips forward, down, up, and around, thus completing a circle and overrolling. Underrolling was the reverse movement.

My name frequently echoed off the walls during that segment of class. "Push, Stephanie! Pull, Stephanie!" Instead of rolling smoothly, my hips would lock, which resulted in short, jerky movements.

I lurched forward like a car driven by an inexperienced driver. As Djalaal walked around the class correcting us, she reminded us that we wouldn't need to take the class if we were already perfect. "The most difficult thing is making it look easy," she said.

After about sixteen weeks, I developed belly-dancing fever. And, yes! I improved. My overrolls and underrolls were rolling along, and my figure eights began to look more like an eight and less like a zero.

Shortly thereafter, Djalaal drafted some of her intermediate students—me included!—to perform at a recital given by Nazaree, one of her former students. Scheduled to perform were Djalaal and her students, along with Nazaree and her crew, Troupe Tunisia. Djalaal called us Bennet Min Sahara, or the Daughters of the Desert. Our recital hall was a restaurant, and we had to make our own costumes.

Making the costume was not my biggest problem. Performing in front of strangers was! When I go to nightclubs, I won't dance unless other people are already on the floor. I have stage fright big time. The closer we got to D-Day, the more my self-confidence quivered and shook. Fearful that I might forget a step, I practiced everywhere—even at the bus stop. Well, I didn't actually practice at the bus stop. I just went over the steps in my head and moved my feet around a little bit. People around me probably thought I either was cold or had to go to the bathroom.

On the day of the show, I had to work, and the restaurant was on the opposite side of town. Travel time was two hours. To save time I made up my face on the bus. Needless to say, I was a nervous wreck.

By the time I got to the restaurant, preperformance jitters along with all the rushing around left me with a bad headache. The midget platoon was tap dancing on my temples and down the nape of my neck. My hands were icy cold, but other than that I was fine.

Backstage, some dancers were scurrying about making last-minute changes. The rest of us just stood staring at all the frenetic activity. "Don't just stand there looking, ladies, practice!" Djalaal yelled. And so we did as best we could in the cramped quarters that also doubled as a dressing room.

Since we were not scheduled to go on until after the intermission, we settled in the back of the restaurant cheering on Nazaree and Troupe

Tunisia. Too soon it was our turn. Evelyn, Kristin, and Karen performed the first number while I waited nervously in the wings. Just before the music to the second number began, I took my place behind Karen. Judgment day had arrived! The music started, and, before I knew it, the dance was over. To this day I don't remember how I made it across the burning sands.

One of the members of Troupe Tunisia told us earlier that our first performance would be like a drug. You don't remember doing it, but later felt "high" from having survived. And she was right. I don't remember much of the dance, but I was still floating when I got home that night.

Aunties and Mamas to the Rescue

Jacqueline Joyner Cissell

"Into each life some rain must fall" is a saying I thought would be with me the rest of my life. After five years of marriage, I was suddenly among the ranks of the single mothers. My son, Joe, was eighteen months old at the time of my divorce and we were on our own. I was dismayed, unemployed, and afraid. For five years I had been a housewife, and now I had to go find a "real" job. I cowered in a bedroom of my stepmother's house until she made me come out and face the world. Even though I might have felt like it, I was never totally on my own, nor have I ever been. I have been blessed with the nurturing, teaching, and comfort of wise, older Black women. My aunties and mamas may not have been related by blood, but they were definitely kindred spirits. These wonderful Black women taught me everything, from grooming and saving money to cleaning the house for the weekend. We also talked about sex. I learned the basics of life from these women. These women have been a constant source of security for me.

One of my mamas, Rose V. Eddington, has shown me a mother's love for as long as I can remember. While I was single and unemployed, Mama would always check to make sure I had food. One day I had to admit that

I just didn't have any. She immediately took a grocery sack from the bottom drawer of the kitchen cabinet and filled it with food from her own supply. That was the first of many things she did for me. One winter, the weatherman warned the area of a coming blizzard. Mama called me and told me to pack a bag and stay with her so I wouldn't be alone during the storm. She and I weathered many storms together. Many days she and I sat together or lay across the bed and talked about any and everything.

After my divorce, I moved back home to central Indiana. I worked two days a week at a local bank and received child support from my former husband; my son and I survived, but barely. A friend and I decided to go to Indianapolis to find a job, and we ended up moving there. I found a job paying $4.13 an hour. The child support paid the rent, the job paid for our food and child care, and Aunt Baby Doll helped me maintain my sanity.

Thank God for a small world! Aunt Baby Doll, also known as Miriam Hall Wilson, and I hailed from the same small town in central Indiana. We had even attended the same church. She agreed to baby-sit my son while I worked. This seasoned Black woman poured much love and instruction into my life; she treated me as if I was one of her own daughters. She cared for my son and fed us both on days when food was scarce.

Aunt Baby Doll also took note of my son's tattered clothes. The little money I paid her for baby-sitting she'd turn right around and use to buy him new clothes. Miriam Wilson raised my son, as I tried to work and provide for him. She is a grandmother to him in every sense of the word.

Aunt Baby Doll taught me about prayer, perseverance, and faith. She shared with me the secrets of motherhood and how to stretch a bag of rice or beans until payday. I loved being around her. Her house was always full of people wanting to talk or eat some of her good food. There was always laughter in her home, and she could crush you on the Scrabble board.

Another woman I must give honor to is Mary Ann Stanley. She also taught me about God and Jesus, how to pray, and how to search the

Scriptures to discover its rich treasures. Whenever I need guidance, whether it is spiritual or natural, no matter what the time is, I can call Mary Ann Stanley. Before I was married, every Friday I would pack a bag and drive about thirty miles to her house and spend many wonderful weekends with her and Pop—her husband, John. He would always look after my car and keep it tied together while Mom Stanley and I would spend time in either the kitchen or in her backyard talking about whatever I wanted to talk about. Mom Stanley is never in a hurry. She patiently listens to me. Many times I have called her to hear her say, "Child, you were just on my mind" or "I was just praying for you."

While I was going through the divorce and many other crises that caused me distress, despair, and uncertainty, these women were my primary support. Sitting under their care and instruction made me feel protected and loved. Their unconditional love and support during some of the most trying times of my life was a blessing from God.

Today I am remarried and have a management position at a local utility. We have a home and two healthy children. I am currently working on a business degree and have been appointed by the mayor to the Civilian Police Merit Board. All of these accomplishments are great, but I arrived there on the prayers and love of these women. Yes, into each life some rain must fall, but the women God sent into my life carried big umbrellas.

A Place to Call My Own
Beverly Phillips McLeod

Most of my life has been spent trying to find my home, a wholesome environment for my color, my spice. My journey began in 1979 with a pilgrimage to Nigeria. There I met my husband, and it was within this intercontinental union that my quest for place intensified to such a feverish pitch that I simply had to find a way to put the issue to rest, once and for all.

Omoragie and I met during my second visit to Nigeria. He was a recent college graduate, I a second-year law student. While I loved his flawless smile and muscular bowlegs, it was our dreams and ambitions that brought us together. We had been harvested from the same crop, so to speak. As we each needed to spend most of our time in our respective home countries, our married life began with us spending time apart. We had identified our needs, but understood little about how to achieve them as a cohesive family unit.

Fourteen years we've shuttled between our entrepreneurial bases of operations in Nigeria and the United States, and every year has been plagued by its own share of emotionally bloody battles. I love my husband, but as I painfully learned over the years, African marital and family customs are not compatible with my needs for identity and home. At

135

every point my husband and I were faced with typical family issues that were exacerbated by cultural dictates and bicontinental living. Property ownership, savings, holidays, children's education, and retirement plans all were constant sources of anger and hostility. We were warlords establishing territorial boundaries. Unfortunately, our rage and frustration often spilled out onto the lives of our young children.

Yet, I've been redeemed by my African experience. Africa offers African Americans a unique and wonderful mirror that reflects the panorama of self untainted by racism. It is a Home where children's dreams are not fractured or restricted by race, but expanded and glorified by land, history, culture, and religion. Through my husband's sharp African resilience I've learned to rebound instead of agonizing over defeat.

Despite all that Africa offers to this wayward daughter, however, I am unwilling to compromise my needs for identity and place. Moreover, I disagree with the African's understanding of me, an African American woman. Here I am, a woman fully grown, with a child by a previous marriage, but in the eyes of Nigerians, I am and always will be my father's daughter. African patriarchal society requires the absolute sanction of male authority on my decisions about my own life. I wanted to be a cherished African wife, but my mother's exhortations encouraging self-sufficiency had filled my way of thinking for too long.

Ironically, Omoragie and I started out as equal partners, an enlightened African couple. We combined our money to capitalize our first company. Although extravagant living was possible in Nigeria, our first few years were like living in a tropical version of Perestroika. Neighbors and veteran "Niger wives," expatriates from lands the world over, counseled, "Make you manage now," words of wisdom gleaned from their many years of hard-won experience.

Every two months I would travel to Nigeria. I'd stay for six to eight weeks, then fly back home to the States. The day finally came when my husband had enough—he refused to buy my airline ticket. Independently, I had no way to return to the United States. I had violated my mother's rule. Trapped, my only bargaining tool was my opposition. In Ishan (my husband's village) we say, *Oria Ono Ne Co Co Sine*—the person you thought would be nothing ends up becoming the person you have to regard. Quietly, I turned our Nigerian home into a spiritless shell, seething with hostility. The tension lasted until the day I finally traveled. That was the last time I stayed against my will.

During recent years, my primary residence has been my home country. Home provides the nourishment I need to accomplish my goals and aspirations. Home is the source of my ideology and my mental well-being. Most importantly, my American home enables me to reconnect with my friends and family. I can deal with family crises at a moment's notice. As in Africa, where a person's family is his/her treasure, I have chosen not to forsake my indigenous family.

Despite the struggle for control over residential identity, Omoragie and I have produced two beautiful children, an industry in Nigeria, and a host of other enterprises spanning three continents. Independent of my husband, I was recently appointed to a political post in California. We are a successful, modern couple, but the cost has been high, paid for in years of mercenary effort.

It's funny. Family and friends in America interpret my business etiquette and mannerisms as Nigerian. My fellow Niger wives see me as a nonconformist. I am truly African American. While my heart still thumps at the sight of Omoragie's sexy legs, I have to remain true to my personal quest. I dare say, I've acquired a sense of entitlement.

Now, after many planting seasons vacillating between contrary clans of thinking, I have finally claimed a place to call my very own.

Breaking the Rules
Shirley Chisholm

The first big event in a freshman congressman's career is his assignment to a committee. He is not likely to get the one he wants because length of service, seniority, counts more than anything else and there are several hundred more senior members ahead of him. But for the sake of courtesy the leaders of his party ask him which one he prefers. Democrats in the House leave the power to assign members to committees in the hands of the fifteen Democrats who form the majority of the Ways and Means Committee. The Republicans have a special Committee on Committees that does the same things. Why they need so many people to do the job is hard to understand. The only criterion that matters in picking members for committee vacancies is their length of service in Congress. Congress calls it the seniority system.

I call it the senility system.

My first choice, naturally, was the Education and Labor Committee, because I am an educator and because I had worked on and for educational legislation in the New York State assembly. There were some vacancies on the Democratic side, and it would have made sense to take advantage of my twenty years' experience in education by appointing me to one of them. Next I would have liked to have been appointed to the Banking and Currency Committee, because it holds the purse strings for housing construction, and, next to education and employment, housing is the major need of poor people, black and white. The Post Office and Civil Service Committee would also have been relevant to my interests to some extent. A large part of post office employees are blacks or from other minority groups. Failing all those, I would have welcomed appointment to the Government Operations committee. I thought it would be a chance to satisfy my curiosity about how government decisions are made and how federal money is spent.

New York's representative on the Democratic committee is Representative Jacob H. Gilbert of the Bronx. He assured me that he would try to get me an education committee seat. I sent a letter with a résumé of my background to every majority member of Ways and Means.

The committee meetings are held behind guarded doors, but it is impossible to keep that many congressmen from talking afterward. I learned by the grapevine that the committee had met and assigned me to the Agriculture Committee. Gilbert assured me he had tried to get me a better assignment, but other members confided that he hadn't tried very hard.

The Agriculture Committee sounded like a ridiculous assignment for a black member from one of the country's most deprived city neighborhoods, but as a matter of fact it might not have been completely out of line. I had grown up on a farm (although I'm sure no one on the Ways and Means Committee knew that when they gave me the assignment; I probably just got what was left over after the other assignments had been made). But more than that, the committee has jurisdiction over food stamp and surplus food programs and is concerned with migrant labor—subjects with which I am concerned and to which I could make a contribution.

Then I found out what my subcommittee assignments were to be:

rural development and forestry. Forestry! That did it. I called Speaker McCormack. The only time I had ever talked to the Speaker was a few days earlier. He had come over to the Capitol Hill Hotel, where I was holding a reception for a large group of people from Brooklyn, to administer the oath of office to me before the group. He had sworn me in earlier that day, with the other first-year members, as the House began its first session of the new Congress, but he had gracefully agreed to come to the hotel and repeat the ceremony for my neighbors and friends, for whom there had not been room enough in the spectators' gallery.

"I don't know if this is protocol, Mr. Speaker," I told him, "but I wanted to talk to you because I feel my committee and subcommittee assignments do not make much sense." John McCormack was cordial and sympathetic. His manners never fail him. Could he help me get my assignment changed to one with some relevance to my district?

"Mrs. Chisholm, this is the way it is," the Speaker said. "You have to be a good soldier."

After I was a good soldier for a few years, my reward would come, he assured me.

"All my forty-three years I have been a good soldier," I said. "The time is growing late, and I can't be a good soldier any longer. It does not make sense to put a black woman representative on a subcommittee dealing with forestry. If you do not assist me, I will have to do my own thing."

The Speaker was startled for the first time. "You what?"

"It means I will do what I have to do, regardless of the consequences. Doing your thing means that if you have strong feelings about something, you do it."

What he thought I meant, I will never know. Probably he was afraid I would start some disturbances. He said he would talk to Wilbur Mills, the chairman of the Ways and Means Committee.

Mr. Mills, the Arkansas Democrat who is absolute ruler of one of the most powerful committees on the Hill, did not like it that a freshman had complained about his assignment, and had even gone over his head to do it. What the two of them said, I never found out, but they agreed to ask Agriculture Committee chairman W. R. Poage of Texas whether I could have a different subcommittee. Mills had been annoyed, but Poage, I heard later, really blew his stack and made some very unpleasant remarks.

There was one avenue of attack left. The committee assignments still had to be approved by the full Democratic majority at a caucus. I appealed to some of the more experienced members for advice on how to move that my assignment be reconsidered. Representative Brock Adams of Washington coached me but warned, "The way they operate, you won't get recognized to make your motion."

He was almost right. Every time I rose, two or three men jumped up. The senior member standing is always recognized first, so they never got to me. They probably expected that I would be discouraged after a while. Men were smiling and nudging each other as I stood there trying to get the floor. After six or seven attempts, I walked down an aisle to the "well," the open space between the front row of seats and the Speaker's dais, and stood there. I was half afraid and half enjoying the situation, as Mr. Mills, who was in the chair, conferred with the majority leader, Carl Albert of Oklahoma. They must have been talking about what to do with me, because after the huddle ended I was recognized.

"For what purpose is the gentlewoman from New York standing in the well?" Mr. Mills asked.

"I'd been trying to get recognized for half an hour, Mr. Chairman," I said, "but evidently you were unable to see me, so I came down to the well. I would just like to tell the caucus why I vehemently reject my committee assignment."

I had a short speech prepared. It said that even though I had spent twenty years in education and served on the Education Committee of the New York Assembly for four years, I understood that geography and seniority make it difficult for a first-term representative to get his first choice of a committee assignment.

"But I think it would be hard to imagine an assignment that is less relevant to my background or to the needs of the predominantly black and Puerto Rican people who elected me, many of whom are unemployed, hungry, and badly housed, than the one I was given."

I pointed out that there were only nine black members of the House, although in terms of the percentage of the population that is black there should be more than forty (I underestimated—I should have said fifty-five). So, I said, the House leadership "has a moral duty to somewhat right the balance by the putting of the nine members it has in positions where they can work effectively to help this nation meet its critical problems of racism, deprivation, and urban decay." Then I offered a resolution removing me from the Agriculture Committee and directing the Ways and Means Committee to come back to the next monthly caucus with a different assignment for me.

My amendment created a parliamentary problem of some kind, and Mr. Mills asked me to withdraw it on the assurance that he would recognize me to offer it later. I did, and he was as good as his word. It passed.

Several of the male members spoke to me afterward in sympathetic terms, as if I had just had a death in the family. "You've committed political suicide," one advised me. That phrase sort of made me feel at home.

"The leadership will have it in for you as long as you're here," I was warned. What puzzled me and made me angry was that some of these men really agreed with me. "You're right, we need change around here," they said. But what they didn't say, and perhaps did not realize they were revealing, was that they didn't dare to fight for it themselves.

It is incomprehensible to me, the fear that can affect men in political office. It is shocking the way they submit to forces they know are wrong and fail to stand up for what they believe. Can their jobs be so important to them, their prestige, their power, their privileges so important that they will cooperate in the degradation of our society just to hang on to those jobs?

At the next Democratic caucus, I was assigned to the Veterans' Affairs Committee, whose chairman, Olin "Tiger" Teague of Texas, had assured me after the first caucus that he would be delighted to have me on his committee anytime. It was an improvement; as I told people, "There are a lot more veterans in my district than there are trees."

Marriage 101
Edward Allen, Jr.

I was married July 27, 1963, to Marie Savage. In this day and age of divorce, I am happy to say we've been married thirty-three years. We've produced three beautiful children—Jennifer, Jonathan, and Jason. How did we do it? What's our secret? Read on!

I love you. The first part of this challenge is the choice of a mate, and obviously, love plays a major role. I met my wife on a blind date and our chemistry simply evolved from there to its highest level. It has continued to grow over the years. And just because we love each other doesn't mean that we don't have our ups and downs. We've learned that marriage requires some give and take on both of our parts.

Space. The No. 1 thing I have found is that people need their own space. When you go into a marriage, clearly your individual life-style requires some adjustments. But, at the same time, you should not infringe upon other people's freedom.

. . .

Share hobbies. There are things that my wife and I enjoyed before we entered this union. We continued this process and respected each other's quality time, so to speak. For instance, she enjoyed bowling. I've been an athlete all my life and football was my pride and joy. She didn't necessarily enjoy watching the games; yet, she went out and bought a book on football so she would at least understand what was going on. I didn't particularly care for bowling, but I learned how anyway. Turns out, I ended up enjoying the game more than she did.

There are a number of things that you try to do together and then there are times when people need their private moments. My wife enjoys shopping; I don't. Sometimes she goes shopping for days. I've learned to let her do her own thing and not infringe upon it.

Agree to disagree. There are times when we've gotten angry at each other, but no matter how mad we get, we always try to discuss things. Most important, when we had a difference in opinion, we never argued in front of our kids. I made that clear up front when we first married. My childhood experiences with my stepfather made me want to find a peaceful way to resolve conflicts. If we had anything to disagree about, we waited until the kids were out of hearing range. What usually ended up happening was that by the time we got a chance to talk, we'd both calmed down.

Money, honey. Another important part of the happy marriage equation is economics. I've always been fortunate enough to provide an income to care for our needs. This allowed my wife to remain home for twenty-five years and care for our children, which is also what she wanted to do. Fortunately, I was able to provide the financial support for her and our children. This type of arrangement definitely made a difference in our children. We're very proud that all three have graduated from college. They've given us nothing but pleasure.

Children. When the first child becomes a part of the household, there is a real adjustment. Obviously, the entire context of your relationship changes. A mother spends a lot more time bonding with the child than the father does. He has to get out and bring home the bacon, the pabulum, and the milk. Also, the intimate part of your relationship changes to some extent. You have to allow a period for your wife to heal before returning to sexual activity. You have to practice a bit of celibacy for humanitarian reasons, if you care about your mate.

Empty nest. When our children grew up and left home our marriage returned to its original state. We were free to do all the things we had done before the children, such as going to a show without buying popcorn for five people and not calling around for a baby-sitter. Actually, you find yourself with an enormous amount of time on your hands. Of course, there is also additional income too; it makes you think that you've really hit the lottery! The best part, though, is getting to know each other again. We spend a lot of quality time together, going on vacations and to social events, that we never had the time to do while raising children. After the housewifing and mothering roles were no longer needed, Marie decided to return to work and graduate school, and I'm proud of her.

One couple under God. God has played a very important role in the longevity of our marriage. Prayer has a place in everything we do. No matter how cynical you may become, you can still look around and see the perfection of God's creation. There must be a greater being than ourselves, and if you believe this, you must put it into practice. You say your prayers, look around, and see some answers. You pray that everything turns out well and if you believe, it occurs. Prayer keeps the marriage rolling. When there is a misunderstanding, if you pray before going to bed, the problem tends to subside. I think it's very important to never go to bed upset with your mate. Ugly things said earlier tend to disappear once you make peace with your mate and your Maker. My wife takes her moment and prays, then I take mine. I would guess in most cases we're both praying about the same things.

Time has gone by so fast. Thirty-three years ago seems like yesterday. Time flies when you're having fun and you love the one you're with.

Taming the Fire Inside
Ben Mtundu

For the past sixteen years, I have been dealing with men's issues—working with men and their anger, helping men to affirm their masculinity in nonshaming, empowering ways, and sharing information on making healthy choices instead of simply reacting to stressful situations.

I understand men's anger because I have been filled with rage for much of my life. Traumatic childhood experiences laid the foundation for this work. All of the male figures in my family—my father, uncle, and grandfather (whom I revered)—were dysfunctional. My father was an alcoholic and very abusive to his family. My grandfather, an alcoholic, died when I was quite young. He was the last role model in my family with whom I shared any connection. My father's brother-in-law, my uncle, for whatever reason, had learned to express himself in an inappropriate sexual way. He raped me when he was fourteen years old. I was seven years old. I believe that he too had been molested.

After my grandfather died, I lived in a household headed by a single female parent. There was a lot of abuse among the siblings. We were quite violent, to put it bluntly.

Like the typical American male, I came of age without any serious nurturing from another male. At twenty years old I was emotionally illiterate and already making babies. Although it wasn't right, the violence I had grown up with was all I knew. The value of "might makes right" was carried over into my adult life and became a sorry part of my first marriage.

My first wife would constantly say that I was crazy and that I needed to be put away. I didn't buy that. I'd worked in a mental institution before—I knew I wasn't crazy. No way was I going to be drugged up and locked down like an animal.

On the other hand, I was abusing her. I was beating her—fighting and choking her because she would piss me off. The last incident that I had with my first wife was on a city bus in Kansas City, Missouri. My youngest son was in her arms, but my anger and rage were so intense that I barely noticed him. All I knew was that she had pushed my button again and I had to deal with that. I fought and verbally abused her. I did this with my son watching.

We were in and out of a relationship for two years. Although much of it was violent, a little glimmer of healing light began to touch my soul. Slowly but surely I began to peel the onion, peeled all the layers back to figure out what I was angry about. I wanted to learn how to stop the abusive behaviors.

Believe it or not, stopping the violence became easy when I learned to focus on controlling my own behavior rather than someone else's. I learned to communicate: "Hey, I need to back off and process. I need to explain to her that I am angry." Or, realizing the situation was beyond my control, I learned to walk away.

I was wrestling with a monster. Abusive behavior is not just physical, but verbal, attitudinal, emotional, and financial. The line between emotional violence and physical violence is very thin, especially if there are past traumas to complicate matters. No way can another person know what words or behaviors will trigger past memories. Sometimes not even the one who has been traumatized knows what will trigger rage and violence.

Needless to say, the healing process was very long because the work I had to do was solely on myself. No one else could come in and do the work for me. I could not be lazy, and at the same time I had to go easy on myself if I got stuck. When I did get stuck and couldn't figure a piece out, I learned to live with ambiguity and confusion, trusting that the answers would eventually come in their own time. Trying to articulate my feelings of confusion was also very important.

Sixteen years later, I'm still processing and connecting what happened to me when I was seven to my present actions. Sometimes I don't want to process but move directly to the results. I often don't want to do the in-between stuff. This is dangerous, not wanting to check out where I am, not feeling but going on automatic pilot. That's something a lot of men do, and I'm no different. What makes me different from men who have not done the hard heart work is that I have tools to help me connect with the emotional stuff that I sometimes want to bypass. Every man owes it to himself to dig deep within his soul and begin the healing process. This takes courage, but our emotional health and the quality of our lives depend on the emotional healing of men.

In the path that I chose I learned about my codependency. I learned about my own dysfunctions as well as my family's. I also learned that the women in my life also had similar issues but from a female perspective. We were all in the same boat.

Several years ago I established the Men's Anger Network. Through this organization I help other men to become conscious of their anger. Anger, believe it or not, is a healthy emotion. It's the smoke detector that lets us know there is a fire inside. To deny such warnings can be fatal to our relationships and our emotional and physical health. Instead of resorting to inappropriate sex, drugs, alcohol, smoking, work, food, or other addictive behaviors, men must begin the slow but necessary growth to finding their self-worth. This is really key for us men.

I advocate for men because, as statistics show, we are the ones who are the most violent in our communities. I have found that in addition to getting in touch with all of my emotions, a spiritual, African-centered approach to life has helped me to become comfortable with myself. I can finally say that I feel good about being an African man.

As African men come together with other African men, the healing force will grow exponentially, embracing us all until we finally are whole. Although intimacy with other men is a taboo in American society, it is absolutely essential to our growth and development. The Million Man March opened the door to this emotional wealth that we have. This brave gathering of brothers allowed us to tap into our emotions and embrace one another and acknowledge the garbage. And that was only the tip of the iceberg. We came back home asking many questions, searching our souls. The gathering reaffirmed my work with the Men's Anger Network.

Many men and young boys have father wounds. These are the wounds that occurred from us not having fathers around. These are the wounds that told us we needed to grieve, find closure, and move on. We will heal as we honestly deal with our father wounds.

My sons grew up with me doing this work. They are the beginning to the end of men not having other men to turn to. I've freed them from their dependence on the umbilical cord, the apron, and the breasts. They can turn to other men and say, "Hey, I am hurting, and I need you to care about that. I need to share that with you, and I'm taking a big risk in doing it, but I'm doing it."

How to Pick a Mango When There's a Lizard in the Way

Hyacinth A. Williams

Climbing has always interested me. I don't see it as a challenge necessarily—just a way to directly reach a goal. Growing up as a child in my native Kingston, Jamaica, climbing trees, especially mango trees, was fun for me. The luscious ripe mangoes hanging by their stems were no challenge for me. Although there were obstacles to be faced and decisions to be made even before I climbed those mango trees that surrounded my home, they never deterred me from obtaining my goal.

When most mangoes are ripe, all that is necessary to get them down off of the tree is a good shake, and they'll come falling to the ground. During rainstorms, mangoes fall off limbs easily. Sometimes, though, it's not so easy to separate a mango from a tree, which means someone has to climb to get it. In my family, that someone was me. Other than Pet, my sister with whom I did many wonderful things, I can't remember my other sisters climbing trees—ever.

Once I saw the mango I wanted, I'd start plotting on ways to get it down. I'd climb up the trunk to a branch that was sturdy enough to hold me without breaking. Inevitably I'd come face to face with a lizard, green or brown in color. As we eyed each other, I did not think that my size alone justified my pursuit. I did not think "I'm bigger, therefore—" I simply had a goal and nothing was going to stop me, not even a lizard. I kept my eyes on the creature and the mango, both. The closer I got to the end of the branch where the mango was waiting for me, the closer I'd get to the lizard, which would stare at me, daring me to pass. We'd stare at each other, then I'd make a small movement forward, causing it to dart away and scurry down the trunk.

All that was left between me and my mango was the weak branch. Leaving the safer, sturdier, thicker part of the branch, I'd move slowly toward my goal. The closer I got to the mango, the thinner the branch became. Slowly, I'd crawl, inching my way to the end of the branch, my sister Pet down below cheering me on. There was real danger at this point because the branch could snap at any moment, and I'd be one broken-up little girl. But I never let fear paralyze me. I just kept moving toward the mango.

As I reached the thinnest part of the branch, I would stoop, lie down, and then stretch. The branch would start swaying to the rhythm of the warm summer wind, but I'd keep stretching until I could finally touch it. My fingers would brush the fruit, I'd get a firm grip, and the mango was in my hand! It was mine! I would throw the prize down to my sister's upreached hands.

Another obstacle faced me. I had to get down from the tree! As quickly as possible I had to retrieve what I had entrusted to my much adored sister. I couldn't allow gravity to pull me down. Well, children can be really brave (or foolish). The lizard now long forgotten, I simply scooted back away from the fragile limb. At this point in my adventure my only concern was getting back down to earth to retrieve the mango out of my beloved sister's greedy hand.

I looked down at my mango, and could taste its sweet, juicy goodness. I stepped up my pace, crawling back the way I had come. That mango was ready to be eaten, and eaten by me! I just had to get that mango.

This time I didn't stoop. Now was not the time for caution. Quickly, I slithered backward, my belly on the thin branch, until I reached the thick, sturdy place. I breathed a sigh of relief, hugged the trunk and carefully slid down to the ground.

I must have really loved my sister to share my precious mango with her. As I peeled the skin and licked the sweet juices from my fingers, I realized that all my efforts were worth it. My mango was ripe, sweet, and juicy—just right. I gave my sister a broad side of the mango and kept the rest with the large seed. As we enjoyed eating together, the juice of the mango ran down our arms to the elbows. We licked it off, looked at each other, and laughed. Oh, the sweet taste of success!

To Boldly Go

Nichelle Nichols

It was after I'd been hired as a member of the *Star Trek* crew, and producer Gene Roddenberry and I conceived and created her, that Uhura was born. Many times through the years I've referred to Uhura as my great-great-great-great-great-great-great-granddaughter of the twenty-third century. Gene and I agreed that she would be a citizen of the United States of Africa. And her name, Uhura, is derived from Uhuru, which is Swahili for "freedom." According to the "biography" Gene and I developed for my character, Uhura was far more than an intergalactic telephone operator. As head of Communications, she commanded a corps of largely unseen communications technicians, linguists, and other specialists who worked in the bowels of the *Enterprise*, in the "comm-center."

In the fall of 1966, *Star Trek* premiered on NBC to a less than overwhelmingly positive response. The debut episode, "The Man Trap," revolved around a shape-shifting, salt-craving monster with the power to assume a form attractive enough to seduce whomever it encounters. To Bones, she is a youthful version of a long-lost love, for instance. Uhura comes close to being attacked by the monster in the guise of a beautiful Swahili-speaking Black man. Fans do not consider this one of the best episodes, but it had its moments. This and other episodes suggest how

Uhura and the other characters might have developed further. Uhura was a new kind of television woman in many ways. Yet even at this early point in the show, it was becoming uncomfortably obvious that whatever ambitious plans Gene had for my character, Uhura's role was constantly being diminished.

There were so many good things about working on *Star Trek*—the money, the exposure, my coworkers—that it was with great difficulty that I resolved to leave after the first season. After we wrapped up the last show, I walked into Gene's office and resigned.

"There's too much here that I just can't take," I explained. "I've put up with the cuts and the racism, and I just can't do it anymore."

Gene listened attentively, then said, "Nichelle, please think about it."

"Gene, you've been wonderful, but there's too much wrong here, and I can't fix it." We talked a while longer, and before I left, we hugged warmly. Then he said, "I don't want you to do this. I can make things better. I do have a problem, and I am fighting a hard battle."

I sensed what Gene had alluded to, but I didn't really know what he was trying to communicate. At this time, I had no idea how far he'd gone to protect me.

"If you leave, they win," he said intently. "And if they chase you away, they win double."

I said goodbye to Gene, thinking to myself that if I stayed and allowed myself to be treated as less of a person than my coworkers, the ubiquitous "they" were winning, too. It simply wasn't worth it to me anymore.

The following evening I attended an important NAACP fundraising event. I was chatting with someone when a man approached and said, "Nichelle, there is someone who would like to meet you. He's a big fan of *Star Trek* and of Uhura."

I turned to greet this "fan" and found myself gazing upon the face of Dr. Martin Luther King, Jr. I was stunned, and I remember thinking, *Whoever that fan is, he'll just have to wait.*

The man introduced us. Imagine my surprise when the first words Dr. King uttered were, "Yes, I am that fan, and I wanted to tell you how important your role is."

He began speaking of how he and his children watched *Star Trek* faithfully and how much they adored Uhura. At that moment the impact of my decision really struck me. Nevertheless, I replied, "Thank you, Dr. King, but I plan to leave *Star Trek*."

"You *cannot*," he replied firmly, "and you *must* not. Don't you realize how important your presence, your character is?" he went on. "Don't you realize this gift this man has given the world? Men and women of all races going forth in peaceful exploration, living as equals. You listen to me: Don't you see? This is not a Black role, and this is not a female role. You have the first nonstereotypical role on television, male or female. You have broken ground—"

"There have been other Black stars," I countered.

"In TV?" he replied. "Yes, Beulah, Amos and Andy. Do I need to go further?"

"No," I answered softly.

"You must not leave. You have opened a door that must not be allowed to close. I'm sure you have taken a lot of grief, or probably will for what you're doing. But you changed the face of television forever. You have created a character of dignity and grace and beauty and intelligence. Don't you see that you're not just a role model for little Black children? You're more important for people who *don't* look like us. For the first time, the world sees us as we should be seen, as equals, as intelligent people—as we *should* be. There will always be role models for Black children; you are a role model for everyone.

"Remember, you are not important there in spite of your color. You are important there *because* of your color. This is what Gene Roddenberry has given us."

All that weekend Dr. King's words echoed in my mind as I weighed every factor. Perhaps he was right: Perhaps Uhura was a symbol of hope, a role model. And if that were the case, did I not owe it another chance? Granted, Uhura's full potential had not been realized, and, sadly, probably wouldn't be. But she was there, wasn't she? And that had to count for something.

When I returned to work on Monday, I went to Gene's office first thing and told him about my conversation with Dr. King and my decision to stay.

A tear came to Gene's eye, and he said, "God bless that man. At least someone sees what I'm trying to achieve."

STEP FOUR

Cooking the Peas

"Black-eyed peas are a down-home food. When I was growing up in Jacksonville, Alabama, your great-grandma, my grandma, would cook 'em in molasses and serve it over rice. She'd cook 'em with ham, pig tails, bacon—whatever she'd have lying around, and she'd cook 'em in a pot as big as this kitchen on that tiny wood-burning stove. We'd be eating black-eyed peas for weeks. Every New Year's she'd cook a batch for good luck."

"Good luck?"

"Right, cook 'em on New Year's and you'll have good luck for the rest of the year," said Daddy.

"Sounds like some superstitious Negro nonsense to me," I said superciliously. But as soon as I said it, I regretted it. My father looked to heaven and shook his head sadly.

"You complain about your son not caring about our history—wonder where he got it from?" I deserved that.

"Daddy, I'm sorry. I didn't mean to crack, but you've got to admit—black-eyed peas, good luck, oh c'mon!"

Daddy sat down in one of the old sturdy chairs. It was such a slow, pained movement, it hurt me to watch. His knees creaked and groaned, and I could tell his back hurt. Must be going to rain. His arthritis was more dependable than the weatherman. I wanted to give him some ibuprofen, but I knew better than to make a fuss. My mother fusses, to his great irritation. So I kept silent, wincing at every creak of the knees.

The salty, smoky smells of the boiling turkey danced with the smooth piano of Ramsey Lewis. Daddy's eyes were closed. He seemed to be listening to the music for strength. He sighed deeply, then said, "Get me a beer." Quickly, I got a can out the refrigerator, popped the top, and poured it for him in a tall, clear glass, making sure to give it a good, foamy head. It was kind of early in the day, but I guess I had driven him to it. Whatever it took to keep his blood pressure down.

I handed him the glass of ale and stoically awaited my tongue-lashing. Instead, he told me to sit down, and then he proceeded to tell me a story. It was a story about how my great-great-grandma had walked off the plantation with my great-grandma in hand and set up housekeeping in Jacksonville. Times were hard, but our family has the work ethic stitched into our genetic code. These brave women used the skills that kept them alive on the plantation and set up a family cooking business—catering, they'd call it today—that fed folks from miles around. With a single, solitary wood-burning stove, they'd cook turkeys, hams, sweet potato pies, pecan pies (there was a huge pecan tree out front), peach cobbler, fried chicken, cheese sticks, pound cake, and the sweetest ambrosia ever concocted by woman.

"There was never an easy time when I was growing up. We had to fight Jim Crow, the Ku Klux Klan, and other Black folks. Sometimes, throwing kernels of corn on the ground with a prayer or fixing a big batch of black-eyed peas on New Year's Day was the only things that gave us hope for a better life. And somehow, some way, we'd manage to get over. That Negro nonsense, as you call it, gave us hope and a laugh when there wasn't nothing to laugh about."

I had been properly chastised. "I'm sorry," I said, my cheeks hot with shame.

"Don't put down something you don't know nothing about," he said. I nodded. "Now let's get back to work," he said.

Our heroine and her teacher load the pot of peas with onions, celery, garlic, peppers, tomato paste, chili powder, and a bay leaf. The turkey wings are laid to the side, and the salty water is used to cook it all. Our heroine is forbidden from measuring anything. She must feel her way through the process. A pinch here, dash there. She turns on the flame, and for three hours, the ingredients will simmer, stew, and blend. She learns that to make a truly excellent pot of peas takes persistence, tenacity, and most of all, a vision.

From Welfare to Self Care

Debora Tutterrow

God bless the child.
I know I have to get my own.
Later for the man with the money.
Later for the welfare.
I'm hellbent on overcoming the myths of the
    Welfare Mother for I am her.
Welfare—the trap and trickbag like no other.

I grew up in a family of five kids. I was the only girl in the family. With four brothers, I was so spoiled and privileged. My dad was a successful hairdresser. He was one of the few men who dared to do hair—perms, no less! He was very popular. My mom had one of those well paying manufacturing jobs that were plentiful back then. As a result, I had everything I needed and a whole lot I wanted. We went on picnics and traveled out of state on vacations every year in our station wagon. We even flew to Los Angeles one year to visit relatives, and the biggest deal was a trip to Disneyland.

In school, I was voted Most Likely to Succeed. I was the swimming champ, cheerleading captain, student leader, Miss Popularity. The same in college. Dean's list, Biomedical Club president, and so on.

So how does a girl go from a wonderful childhood and an all-American upbringing to welfare recipient, single mother of two?

How did I become a resident of the police district with the highest homicide rate in town?

How did I get to 13th and Millard, a building in one of the most notorious neighborhoods in Chicago?

I made my mistakes in life like everyone else; however, my mistakes cost me too much in time, money, and my self-worth. What was my crime that sentenced me to hard time on the welfare line? I got pregnant! More to the point, I trusted him! Aha!

I was a junior at a prestigious college in Chicago when I became pregnant with my youngest daughter. I was living with her father and our three-year-old girl at the time. He suggested that I take a break from school and resume my studies after the baby was born. Since I'd only miss one semester, it sounded like a good enough idea to me at the time. I listened to him.

After my daughter was born, I was very content. Just a regular little ol' happy homemaker. However, I soon grew restless and ready to finish school, but he felt there was no need for me to rush. I could go back when the girls got bigger, he said. He really did not like the idea of the kids being with a sitter when they could have their mommy. He said that he made enough money to take care of us and that a lot of women would love to be able to stay home with their families. It made sense to me. I agreed with him. I trusted him.

A couple of years later, I discovered that while I was making a home for him and our family, he was out running the streets, getting busy with any and every woman he could find.

Devastated, I left and took my girls with me. Good-bye to the five-bedroom home, the shopping trips, and his whole paycheck in my hand every two weeks. Hello, welfare. I was what they call a displaced housewife. Really, I was a housewife who wasn't about to take any more you know what. All I had were my children, about $3,000, and the car he bought me for Mother's Day.

I was mad at myself for having been so gullible. Now here I was, single with two kids, no college degree, no income, no skills whatsoever. I couldn't even type! All I knew how to do was cook, clean, and take care of kids. That's what you call a funky situation.

We lived from pillar to post, from relatives to friends until I could find a decent place. That was a very difficult thing to do, because a lot of places did not accept children. Apartments were either too expensive or too raggedy. No middle of the road to be found. After a few months of that unstable action, I finally found an apartment in a subsidized re-habbed building on 13th and Millard. This building largely housed single mothers on welfare and some senior citizens.

Still, I was grateful. The first thing I did when I set foot in the apartment with my own keys was to fall down on my knees in prayer to thank God for this blessing. I asked Him to bless my home and to give me strength. I had no idea how much strength I was going to need.

I stayed in that apartment for four years. I made a lot of good friends whom I love dearly to this day and I became sort of a Big Sister in the Hood. Every time I looked around, my name was being called for something. They talked to me about the smallest to the biggest of their problems. They could count on me for a few extra food stamps, a drive to the grocery store, a phone (I was one of the rare tenants with continuous telephone service), small loans, and baby-sitting. I usually left my back door unlocked, so all of the little kids in the building were free to run in and out. The women in the building also returned the same favors to me. We stuck together and worked together like sisters. We were like a big family with a whole lotta kids.

These women depended on me, not because I was better than them, but because I had more formal education, which enabled me to manage my household better. I had been places in my life. I had seen more and my scope was not as limited as my friends'. However, not even my education and resourcefulness could have prepared me for some of the requests that were made of me.

"Debora! Call the police, my boyfriend poured lighter fluid on my baby! He gettin' ready to set him on fire!"

"Debora, watch out! The police 'bout to break your window. They after Deena's stepbrother. He just tried to rape her and he just threw his gun in your garbage!"

One morning before I could even get out of the door, a friend called me. "Debora, call the police! Aaron is upstairs beating Tina with the cable TV cord and you know she pregnant!" Another neighbor ended up calling the police. As they marched Aaron past my apartment in handcuffs, Aaron yelled, "Debora, call my sister! Tell her what police station I'ma be at!"

To survive in that kind of environment involves much more than knowing how to fight or cuss. You've got to be able to think fast on your feet. It takes knowing when to mind your own business or when to handle your own business. I learned by watching the oldest survivors in the area, the senior citizens. After all, they had been handling their business a mighty long time.

After so many nights and days of that chaos, I decided that the best way to help my friends, myself, and my girls would be to set an example. I would go to school, get a job, and move away! Now I knew I did not have time to finish my degree because I had to get out ASAP. Besides, the public aid system totally discourages you from attending college with all of their insane regulations. No matter, I had a plan. Trade school was the only option. To me it would be a quick getaway. I decided to take a trade, land a job with a company that paid tuition reimbursement, and then finish college later. I could no longer take being Big Sister in the Hood.

I found out about a jobs training program offered by the city that provided childcare and transportation costs. As I was going over the list of vocations, Telecommunications Technician Trainee caught my attention. One of the brothers in my Bible study group was a Telecom Engineer, and he told me a long time ago that computers and telecom networking is the future and that jobs were plentiful. I decided to go for it.

Seemed like as soon as I started my serious effort to change my life things got even more bizarre. There was a fire in our building the night before my first day of class. I was so tired I could barely stay awake in class. The instructor didn't care. He was former military and took no stuff. The class was structured to psychologically condition people like myself who had never been in the workforce or who had been out of it for a while. I had to be there from 8:30 A.M. to 4:30 P.M., just like a job. No lateness or absenteeism was tolerated. I also had three hours of homework a night.

Going to school, raising two kids by myself, and living in that war zone drained me physically and emotionally. Then on top of everything, my car died and right in the middle of a Chicago winter. I had to get up extra early to walk six blocks in the snow and deep freeze weather to take my daughters to the sitter. We had to walk to the laundromat and the grocery store. One day, feeling disheartened and discouraged, I recalled something I had seen one of my elderly mentors do the previous summer.

It was a hot day, about 92 degrees. Gracie was walking up the street with four grocery bags and was breaking a slight sweat. Now at the time, Gracie was 76 years old. I said, "Gracie, you been to the store, huh? Which one?" When she told me Jumbo's, I was speechless. Jumbo's was seven blocks away! Damn! If Gracie, at 76 years old, could walk in the burning hot sun seven blocks each way and come back with grocery bags and not complain, I knew what I had to do. I had to handle my business.

I finished trade school and landed my first job as a telecommunications technician for a small phone-pager sales and repair shop. I hardly ever got paid. Something like $25 a day when I did. It was cool, though, because the money supplemented the aid check. Actually, I was happy and grateful for the opportunity to apprentice under an experienced journeyman. I was getting valuable experience and was being taught wiring by the best.

After nine months of working with that young entrepreneur, I landed a better job at a big corporation. Another excellent foot in the door of opportunity. Only paid about $250 a week, but to me that was progress and it was a real chance to step up my skills. I was a hard worker, so when a better-paying position became available I was ready and able. My only problem was fatigue. I was going to work tired all of the time because I never got proper rest. My boss used to think I was a party animal. Far from it.

No way could I ever get them to understand my living conditions. It was so outrageous, even to me. I didn't think they'd believe me anyway. No sleep because of the shooting and shouting all night. Sometimes I'd look out my peephole and see a drug transaction going on right outside my door or someone throwing up bad dope. The worst was seeing a dead body lying on the ground outside my window. Drug dealers, murderers, and dope fiends had taken over. I was terrified and I hated that my kids were being exposed to all this.

One day my ex came over to visit the kids. There were so many empty dope bags lying on the steps, he just stared at them. He inhaled the pissy hallway smell. He looked full of remorse and guilt. Later that night he called me. He opened his home to me and the kids. He said we could stay there with him until we could find us something better. He told me to think about it and get back to him. Let me tell you I was ready to go right that second, but I just played it off and said okay. I called him the next day to tell him we were on the way. I swear, I left damn near everything I owned there. All I took was our clothes, the kids' bunk beds, and toys. I left a whole house full of furniture behind and didn't care. All I knew was that we had an escape hatch and we were OUT! We stayed with him two months. It was strictly platonic. He was just being a friend and a concerned father, nothing more.

As soon as I saved enough, I signed the lease on a one-bedroom apartment in a luxury high rise downtown on the lake. I had to get as far away from that madness on 13th and Millard as I could. I could barely afford the apartment, but I felt I had to go for it. All I knew was that I just wanted us to be safe. God was with me. The words of a song by the Sounds of Blackness inspired me to keep going: "As long as you keep your head to the sky, stay optimistic." Or, like my cousin Gabrielle likes to say, "You may fall down, but if you land on your back you can still see up."

My skin has been thickened by my experiences. Corporate cut-throats don't even faze me. I just keep studying, refuse to play their games, and work hard to earn respect. I am very determined. I've put the work ethic I acquired in the ghetto to good use to keep progressing. Five years after completing trade school, I have a career as a computer network engineer. In one week, I make three times the amount I received in a month when I was on welfare. I can live almost anywhere I want. My oldest daughter is a happy, well adjusted teenager who is a Principal's Scholar at her high school. The youngest child is ten years old and is a lead dancer in a popular African dance company.

Recently, I treated my daughters and myself to a vacation in Barbados. While there, we had quite a symbolic experience that, for me, reaffirmed my achievements. One evening we toured a former slave plantation. I was struck by how much my former life paralleled that of my slave ancestors. Ironically, the Big House is now a restaurant and art gallery. I used the opportunity to talk about the hell and destruction of slavery. As we dined and I accepted the check for our $100 meal, I contemplated my surroundings. The word "overcome" came to mind. A very important word in the vocabulary of my life. The other thing that was going through my mind was, If massa only knew who came to dinner tonight!

Watchi

(Ghanian Black-Eyed Peas and Rice)

2 lbs. black-eyed peas (soaked overnight)
4 tbsp. oil
salt (to taste)
½ lb. rice
1 cup vegetable oil
3 tbsp. whole wheat flour (heaping)
3 large onions (sliced)
2 cups tomato paste
1½ tbsp. nutmeg (level)

1. Cook peas with the 4 tbsp. oil until almost done.
2. Add salt to taste.
3. Add rice to black-eyed peas.
4. Allow to steam.
5. Reduce heat; simmer until done.

SAUCE
1. Heat the cup of oil in skillet.
2. Add flour, stir until brown.

3. Add onions, cook until brown.
4. Add tomato paste and stir until well cooked.
5. Add water according to desired thickness. (*It should not be soupy.*)
6. Add nutmeg, allow to cook.
7. Sauce is served over black-eyed peas and rice with salad, greens, or any vegetable.

Yields: 20–25 Servings

My Father, John Norton
Ken Norton

My father, John Norton, is in fact my stepfather. He married my mother, Ruth, when I was three, but he treated me and raised me like I was his own.

He was the kind of man who said what he meant and meant what he said. There was no interpretation to his words and his word was the law in the Norton household.

This man, my father, stood only 5'6" and had lost a leg in an unfortunate accident, but he was every inch a man and could get around quite easily. He didn't feel sorry for himself and he still went to work every day at the Jacksonville, Illinois, Police Department as a dispatcher.

I, on the other hand, was blessed with natural God-given talents and never had to work hard for anything. My parents, who were above average financially, worked especially hard to give me the "extra" things in life they hadn't had.

When I was fourteen, I stood 5'11" and weighed somewhere in the neighborhood of 160 pounds. I stood five inches taller than my father and was feeling rambunctious and challenged my diminutive father to a fight.

"Are you sure?"

"Yes, sir," I said out of respect, though I was still going to go through with the fight.

"Then put up your hands," said my father.

As my hands started to come up, my father popped me in the mouth so fast that I didn't know what hit me. I was on the ground in no time. My father picked me up and dusted me off and didn't say another word. He wasn't angry or mad at me. He must have felt as if I had learned my lesson for the day—and I had.

All my life I was involved with sports and chasing the ladies. I never had to study to make good grades. Everything I did was easy. The result was that I was a spoiled brat, an only child who had always been protected, always got what I wanted. When it came time for me to pick a college, I chose one close to home because of a deep lack of inner confidence. I chose a small school, Northeast Missouri State, even though I was offered full scholarships to much bigger schools, among them Miami, Northwestern, Illinois, Michigan, and Missouri.

I stayed only two years at Northeast Missouri State and didn't feel I was getting anywhere. In reality, I was drifting. It was then that I decided to join the Marines. I felt that if anything could turn me into a man, it was the Marines.

I decided to play football in the Marines to get out of reveille and other monotonous activities. You see, if you were an athlete in the Marines, you were treated especially well and got certain privileges. Again, I was looking for the easy way out.

Politics soon reared its ugly head in the Marines. A white officer just happened to be playing the same position as I was—halfback. The only difference was, I was much better and he was playing first string. I was a grunt, he was an officer. I felt that on the football field, rank had no authority, but it did, and so I quit.

As I was walking away from the football field, I walked across the gym where several boxers were hitting the speed bag and shadow boxing. A man named Pappy Dawson saw me and asked me if I might want to give boxing a chance.

"Why not?" I said casually. "If it'll keep me out of reveille in the mornings."

I took to the sport like a duck to water. I won the Marine championship three years in a row and won the Pan American Trials in 1967. When it came time for me to be discharged from the Marines, I entered into a pro career.

The Marine Corps taught me who I was and what color I was. I didn't know I was black. But in the Corps everything is on a one-on-one basis, and I found out what color I was, and it made me proud to be black.

I thought that as a professional boxer, the money would be rolling in. I was 30-1, but was barely making it on $100 a week. Add to that equation a newborn son that I was taking care of (Ken Norton, Jr.) and a mother who left me to take care of him. Financially, I couldn't handle the situation. At one time, I even contemplated robbing a liquor store to make ends meet, but I credit my upbringing with preventing me from committing such a criminal act.

In desperation, I called home to my father and asked to come home. All of my life I had wanted to get as far away as possible from Jacksonville, Illinois, because advancement for a black man was nil. Once I went back, I knew I would be stuck there for the rest of my life, but I was content with that decision once I made that phone call to my father. His answer surprised me.

"No," said my father. "Ken, if you quit now, the next hard thing that comes along you'll quit that, too. No, you stick with boxing. You've got to finish something. Finish this."

It wasn't but a few months later that I had the opportunity to fight Muhammad Ali on March 31, 1973, in which I upset him in a 12-round decision, breaking his jaw in the process. Overnight, I was a sports legend and eventually became a millionaire from my years in the boxing ring. As a former world heavyweight champion, I've been able to embark on a movie career, travel the world, meet famous people, and experience many wonderful things in life.

Had my father, John Norton, sent me that money to bring me back to Jacksonville, Illinois, I probably would have become a police officer. Not that there's anything wrong with that, but my life would not be what it is today—a very fulfilled life!

Most of all, I'm grateful for my wonderful parents, specifically my father. To me, his is a shining example of what a father should be: stern but fair, a man of his word, hard-working, generous, and a leader of the family. The world would be a much better place if everyone had a father as wonderful as mine.

Teaching Self-Worth Through Dance

Ruth Beckford

When in 1947 I approached the Oakland Recreation Department for a job, I was told that they were not hiring anymore playground directors, but they were looking for someone to lead the children in rhythmic classes.

"Rhythmics? What do you mean exactly?" I asked.

"We want someone who can teach children to move freely to music," said general supervisor Carol Pulcifer.

"Do you mean like modern or creative dance?" My heart was beginning to pound. All my life I had been a dancer. I'd danced with Katherine Dunham. I was the first Black to be accepted into several Bay Area dance troupes. If I knew nothing else, I knew dance.

"That's it! Can you do that?"

Bells went off. "Yes," I said, trying to maintain a calm facade, "I'm very experienced in it and would love to do it."

"Now, we've never tried this before. In fact, no recreation department in the country has ever done this before."

"I know I can do it," I said. Doubt never entered my mind. I gave them my dance history starting at age three, and at the tender age of twenty-one, I was hired on the spot to teach modern dance for the Oakland Recreation Department.

My first challenge was to introduce modern dance to the community. My supervisors scheduled a series of lecture demonstrations because neither the kids, parents, nor recreation leaders knew what modern dance was. I knew that my "show" would not only have to inform, but persuade. I'd have to make modern dance look like so much fun, so exciting, that the kids would be begging their parents to let them dance.

My lecture demos were held deep in the West Oakland community, at the New Century Center at Fifth and Peralta, the Alexander Center at Fourth and Linden, and Bay View Village, a housing project on West Grand and Cypress.

My second challenge was to win the students' confidence. I decided on the honest approach, let the chips fall where they might. I walked into the gym at the New Century Center. It was still musty from the basketball game that had been played the night before. I changed into my leotards, walked before a small, curious crowd of children, mostly girls, and a smattering of adults. It wasn't exactly the Apollo, but I gave them my all. I took three deep breaths, then I danced and talked about the art I loved. When I was finished, the crowd clapped politely. I bowed and smiled, then walked to a sign-in table, sat down and waited for all comers.

Gradually, a line of girls formed before me. One by one, they gave me their full names, a charming Southern custom. I would have to remember to call the girls by their first and middle names. There had been an influx of Blacks to West Oakland from the South during World War II to work in the defense plants. And while they did find work, unfortunately, children were often left alone while their parents, who worked night shifts, slept during the day. In time, my classes would become a lifeline for many of them.

My leotard and skirt, my Northern accent and, of course, my dance skills, had grabbed their attention, and the girls stayed. In fact, the classes filled in one day.

I began to formulate my own philosophy for the department that very first night of demonstrations. I noticed that playgrounds had well-structured sports activities for boys, but girls' free time was not as well planned. Organized team sports for girls were not popular after school hours, and interest in gymnastics had not begun to flourish. Dance was really the only structured physical workout alternative for girls who were not interested in sports. Thus, I decided to teach dance to girls only. I wanted to have heart-to-heart talks, and there was no way girls could talk freely around boys. My motto became, "Train young girls to be proud women through dance." I knew some of my teachings in culture and the social graces would go against much of what these girls were learning and seeing in their own homes and neighborhoods. It would be important for me to understand their fears to help them develop the courage to make lifestyle changes. I definitely had my work cut out for me.

For many of the girls whose lives revolved around the goings on of Seventh Street, my classes were the highlight of their weeks. Many came from one-parent, low-income families. Not only did they have my undivided attention, but I encouraged them to express their ideas. This was a challenge, because back home they were constantly hushed by parents and teachers. Some days we would simply sit on the floor in a circle and talk about what had happened that day. Slowly, they learned to express themselves in both word and dance, and I was gratified to see them bloom like the pansies in my father's garden.

I was obsessed. I wanted to instill a sense of worth and a positive attitude that had been taught to me by my parents. Every child in the world should hear, "You are God's most whole and perfect child," my mother's beautiful affirmation for me. Those few words have given me a most charmed life. Mama said that when she was pregnant with me, she would pat her stomach and constantly repeat, "You are God's most whole and perfect child." Growing up, I believed my success was a foregone conclusion. I knew I could do anything if I worked hard at it. Thus, my belief in my ability began at a much higher level than my girls who, too often, had been raised in environments of low, or no, expectations and where failure was the presumed outcome of any endeavor.

I demanded that my girls speak politely and with respect for each other's feelings. One day, a girl in my six-to-eight-year-old group shouted, "Here comes ol' fatty Betty." Entering the double doors at the far end of the school auditorium was Betty. She was eight years old and a true chubbet. She was more than twenty pounds overweight, and each roll of fat on her torso stretched her black leotard to the ripping point. Her thighs and arms were filled like sausages in tight casings. She was never without a bag of potato chips or a candy bar in her hand. She was shy and painfully aware of her size. She really liked to dance, though. Betty was light on her feet, surprisingly, and was consistent in her attendance.

"Fatty, fatty, fatty," the rest of the class chanted. I was appalled.

"Ladies, I think we need to talk. Come over here and sit on the floor," I said in a deliberately calm voice.

Oblivious, the girls sat down. "Now, girls, is it nice to call some one out of their name?"

"No, Miss Beckford," they said.

"Would you like someone to call you out of your name?" I asked. I could tell my point was beginning to dawn on them.

"No, Miss Beckford."

"Then I think we owe Betty an apology, don't you?"

"Yes, Miss Beckford."

"Well?"

"We're sorry, Betty," they said.

"And what do you say, Betty?"

The poor thing said quietly, "You're excused."

"Now, ladies, so that we won't forget and call anyone else out of their names, we need to go home and think about our little talk today."

"We don't get to dance, Miss Beckford?" they groaned.

"No, we don't."

"But our time isn't up yet." Tears were beginning to form in some of their eyes.

"Oh yes it is," I said firmly. "You cut it short when you were acting ugly. You're all too pretty to act ugly, so I'll see you all looking and acting beautifully next week."

We quietly dressed and left. A more somber, disappointed group couldn't be found in all of Oakland, but they had learned a valuable lesson: cruel behavior would not be tolerated in my classes.

Another thing that I had to get straight from the start was class wear. The girls would often come to class dressed in shorts over swimsuits. I knew that pride in their dance would be strengthened if the students dressed in leotards. I found a mail order house that gave a good discount on leotards and asked the department to support my plan to get the parents to buy them. A clear, pleading letter was sent to each parent stating the price and deadline for the money. The response was excellent. Parents told me they would sacrifice to buy the leotards because their girls were having such a good time dancing.

"Miss Beckford said" stories started coming back to haunt me soon after I started the classes.

"Miss Beckford said, 'Ladies don't fight.'"

"Miss Beckford said, 'Ladies always have clean fingernails.'"

"Miss Beckford said, 'If you're going to wear nail polish it must be perfect, so it's really less trouble if girls your age don't wear it.'"

Because the students had a special relationship with recreational leaders they didn't have with their teachers or parents, my ability to influence their habits was very strong. Mothers were pleasantly surprised when longtime habits, such as nail biting and finger sucking, suddenly stopped. I'd tell a girl in a minute, "You must stand on the back row until you have stopped biting your nails. I don't like to see your beautiful hands in your mouth." That would fix her, because all dancers love the prestigious front row. Sure, she'd pout, but after a few days she'd say proudly, "Look, Miss Beckford, my nails are growing." I would make a big thing of studying each finger slowly and carefully. "You know, I think I do see a little improvement. You may stand on the next to last row," I'd say. Her eyes would light up with pride. She'd eventually make it to the front row. When everyone was on line I would automatically rotate the rows so that all felt equal.

The classes were free of charge, and we consistently had a long waiting list. So I made up the rule that if the girls missed class without an excuse three times or if they acted ugly after they had been corrected, they would be replaced by a girl on the waiting list. That way I had the luxury of teaching students who were there because they really wanted to be there, not because someone forced them to come.

Open House classes gave the girls' families and friends a chance to share in the classroom experience, mistakes and all. I would greet the audience, and then explain the responsibilities of being a good audience. Black folks tend to be excruciatingly hard on each other, especially on stage artists, and I did not want anyone to shame, embarrass, or humiliate my girls with talking, laughing, or any other show of disrespect. My girls had worked too hard in developing dance skills and building self-esteem. I told the audience, "I teach the girls that a good audience is attentive and polite in that they don't laugh at someone's mistakes and that they show their appreciation by applause." I tried to slip my rules in through the back door, so to speak. It worked. The girls bowed at the end, and our first Open House was a complete success and led to many, many more.

Today, I am proud to say that many of my "daughters" have gone on to be professional dancers with master's degrees in dance. Most importantly, they have grown to be good, strong, confident African American women.

Ultimately it doesn't matter how you get your message across—whether through sports, academics, or dance. Whatever the method, it is important that we pass on morals and values in our youth, to plant seeds so that they can lead productive and happy lives.

Me and the Heartbeats

Yvonne Butchee

By the time I turned forty-one, my life had turned completely around. My twenty-year marriage had come to an end and I had moved from a five-bedroom home in a nice quiet community to a one-bedroom apartment by the expressway. I questioned my decision to leave my marriage and venture out on my own many times, but always came up with the same conclusion—I had done the right thing! My only regret was that it had taken me so long. I felt as though I had wasted many valuable years of my life *and* my ex-husband's.

Feeling the need to do something meaningful, I applied for a part-time job working with young girls in a public housing complex in Chicago. I met with the private funder and the Social Services Director of the community agency I would work out of. To my amazement (I always underestimate my skills), I got the job! My elation soon turned to absolute fear and I was momentarily paralyzed. What on earth did I have to offer these girls? I've never been poor (my parents may have been, but I never was), I've never lived in a city, let alone public housing, and I've never been a parent. Scared out of my wits, I grabbed every book, article, and video that I could get my hands on and started formulating lesson plans and activity sheets. I interviewed the staff at the community center

184

and got recommendations for group members. I made notes. I listened intently. I became more scared than I was before!

Soon the time came for me to meet the girls. Nervous perspiration poured from my armpits while I tried to appear calm and in control. Barely into my meeting, I discovered that they had gotten a copy of the notes I had made during my interviews with the center staff, and had copied and distributed them throughout the community. One of their mothers was particularly angry and had even come to the center to file a complaint. I, too, was angry because I couldn't believe the staff had been so careless in their handling of confidential information. Anyway, I decided that the best way to handle the situation was to be honest, and I was. To my surprise, their anger subsided and our conversation turned to other things. Lo and behold, we were okay! This, I believe, was the foundation for our relationship which has thrived over the last four and one half years.

I chose girls based on our conversations and my gut feelings. I interviewed approximately twenty-five girls, knowing that I could only accept twelve. Decisions came surprisingly easily, however, and soon I had a core of seven girls. They recommended and interviewed additional girls and, with my guidance, selected five new members. We were now a group of twelve with a team leader, but no name. After days of going back and forth, we finally agreed on The Twelve Heartbeats. The name, of course, is a takeoff from the movie *The Five Heartbeats* by Robert Townsend. It seems that the girls were impressed by the friendship and the loyalty displayed by the main characters in the movie and wanted their group to be about the same things. Suddenly, my life took on a whole new direction and I embarked upon a learning experience that would change my entire philosophy of friendship and relationships. It was then that I realized that I was the lucky one.

Over the next few months we spent time developing group guidelines, doing different activities, going to various restaurants, having sleepovers at my house, and generally getting to know each other. This was harder than it sounds, because these girls have a steel guard over their hearts that is very hard to penetrate. I soon learned that the construction of this guard begins shortly after birth and hardens throughout their lives. They then pass the guard on to their children. There is no hugging, no holding, no outward displays of affection. Caring takes the form of hand slapping, arm jerking, and yelling—mostly, "don't," "stop," and "no!" Baby bottles are filled with Pepsi and Kool-Aid and oftentimes potato chips and cookies are pacifiers used to stop babies from crying. No harm is intended. This is how they were raised and this is the only way they know how to raise their children. Sadly, they are only children themselves.

I figured the best that I had to offer them was my honesty, my consistency, and a good example. This meant that I couldn't curse if I expected them not to. I couldn't be late if I expected them to be on time. I couldn't lie and make up excuses. I had to follow through with promises and commitments. In other words, I had to show them all that I was asking them to be. This is, by far, the hardest thing I have ever had to do in my entire life. Even at my father's funeral I could have been a screaming maniac if I had so chosen. Everyone would have understood and even excused my behavior. But not now. I had to be the person I was demanding that they be. And I had to learn to do all this with love.

Loving them was the easy part. They were just children. Being someone they could love was the hard part. I was part of the world that had let them down, that had disappointed them over and over again. I was an adult who didn't live in their community and who didn't know anything about what that means. In their minds, I was someone who was with them because I got paid—just like many of their teachers. As far as they were concerned, I was just another "do-gooder" who told them what *not* to do.

We've struggled over the four and one half years, and the struggle continues. Only there are fewer of us now—five regulars and a couple of hanger-oners. Some graduated from high school; others didn't. Most of them had a baby and some of them had two. I've had to call DCFS Protective Services on one of the mothers and later on take her daughter and son to visit her in a treatment center. I've taken girls to school to try to get them reinstated after expulsions for fighting. I've attended baby showers, graduations, and funerals. I've watched them flounder, and I've watched them excel. I've said good-bye and kept in touch with the one who went off to college. It has been difficult to know when to step in and when to step out. But the hardest part has been in accepting that, though I love them with all my heart, many of them have made, and will continue to make, decisions that will make life harder for them and there is nothing I can do about it. I can only be there after the fact. Strange though it may sound, the comfort is in knowing that they know I will be there.

We've added some younger sisters and cousins to our group, for prevention and preservation. Soon the original members will be adults and will move on with their lives apart from The Heartbeats. Before they leave, however, I will provide for them the opportunity to give whatever they can to the younger girls. My thinking is that a couple of lights will go on in both the younger and the older heads and something special will happen. Maybe I won't ever get to see it, but that's not important. Believing that the possibility exists is what's important.

More than anything, I want them to learn the art of dreaming. Right now I refer to them as sleepwalkers. They move through life with their eyes closed, with no sense of direction, and a very limited vision of tomorrow. They sometimes think of things they'd like to be, but they dare not strive for fear of failure. If they just hang with the crowd, no one will really notice. As I start work with the younger girls, I find I'm much wiser and much stronger, and together we can weave some dreams and build some wings so they can learn to fly.

Pictures on the Wall
Moni Azibo

The year was 1968. The place was the Black community of East Palo Alto, California. The event was yet another act of vandalism and theft against the community's private school, The Day School. During the night, thieves had broken into the school and had stolen typewriters, calculators, copy machines, and everything else they could sell.

The children of the elementary school were stunned and frightened as they walked through the classrooms that morning, seeing the destruction done by the vandals and noting the absence of the familiar school equipment and supplies—all ripped off by unknown assailants under the cover of night.

Like so many IBIs (Independent Black Institutions) during the sixties, The Day School had been attacked by arson, theft, and vandalism several times by vicious diabolical agents afraid of the rock-solid power that comes whenever Black people combine their resources to educate their own. Among the adults—faculty, staff, parents, and concerned community members—morale was low, and more than one was heard to ask, "Will it ever stop?"

But a burning endurance, a persistent passion, an undying faith in our ability to win burned within the soul of David, a teacher who had been at the school since the first day. That very morning he wrote a poem for the students to lift their morale and to teach them the significant lessons of keeping things in perspective, strengthening the faith, and above all, never losing sight of our goals.

David called his poem, "Pictures on the Wall." He wrote about the school's equipment and supplies that had been stolen. And, yes, it would require several thousand dollars to replace them. But he breathed a sigh of relief to know that the thieves had not taken the most valuable asset of the school, so valuable that they were priceless—*the pictures on the wall.*

These were pictures of our present and past heroes—Marcus Garvey, Malcolm X, the Honorable Elijah Muhammad, Harriet Tubman, Jesse Owens, Benjamin Banaker, Nat Turner, Rosa Parks, and many others. Black men and women who had struggled—some of them still in the thick of the struggle—for our survival and progress as a people. Their images on the walls of the classrooms were an ever-present source of strength, guidance, and inspiration. Their faces reflected the truth of our spiritual and physical endurance as a people and our noble strength and beauty as a race. What child's soul did not glow with pride as he glanced up to see the regal stance of Marcus Garvey calling us all to rise up as the noble race we are, or the piercing eyes of Harriet Tubman, determined and unshakable with the strength of an unconquered giant and the cunning of a fox in her repeated journeys to freedom?

Without typewriters, calculators, or microscopes, school opened as usual that morning. After reading and discussing "Pictures on the Wall," students were beaming with pride as they looked at the pictures on the wall and understood the true differences between mere objects of use and the images of inspiration.

How often in life we get bogged down or depressed and find ourselves victims of "thieves"—whether physical, spiritual, or emotional. But the real inspiration to carry on in spite of a setback is not to figure out how much it will cost to replace our "objects of use," but to count our blessings if we still have the "Pictures on the Wall."

Planting Seeds in My Nieces' Garden
Darline R. Quinn

After talking to so many females with men problems and low self-esteem, I decided long ago that my young cousins, as well as all young females, needed to be taught that they were queens and not inferior. Whenever possible, I would plant seeds.

I have some young cousins—Andrea, twelve years old, and Christina, nine, who, when younger, used to spend the weekends at my house quite frequently. Realizing how precocious they were even then, I made up my mind that there was no time like the present to start making them aware of their beauty and inherent queenly rights. I talked to them about being royal heirs of God.

There were always many questions and discussions. You couldn't just tell them something and let it drop. The first time I told them that they were queens, they asked, "Why do you say that?"

I told them that their beauty comes from being an heir of God and that they deserved the best. They deserved the best treatment and consideration from young boys and later on from husbands. I told them that they should carry themselves as somebody special, because God does not make junk. So it became a ritual. Whenever they came over, we would

190

discuss inner beauty and self-worth. They learned that in girl-boy and man-woman relationships, they were to be cherished, appreciated, loved, treated kindly, and protected. They asked me what those words meant, and I answered as best I could. Andrea would listen and give me that intense look she still possesses. Christina, who is more vocal, would talk a little then wait to see what her sister had to say. I often wondered if I was reaching them, but I continued to plant seeds.

One weekend the girls and I were talking and Andrea said to me, "You know what, Darline?"

"What, baby?"

"Bernice's husband is really good to her," she said. Now, Bernice was the mother of Andrea's best friend. Bernice had just given birth to twin boys. I asked her why she said this about Bernice's husband.

Andrea looked at me thoughtfully and said, "He is so nice. He asks if he can do something for her, he asks if she needs anything when he goes to the store, he helps her with the laundry. He sweeps the floor. He says, 'Honey, can I get you anything?' He is just nice."

She had noticed so many of the little things that I was filled with joy. She got it! She had been listening to me all along! I thanked God and was delighted and happy that she was learning how to recognize and appreciate good men. Through Bernice's example, she saw in action, not just principle, a woman being treated like royalty.

And I learned a valuable lesson, too. I learned to trust my intuition, even when the physical reality presents a different picture from my intention. To be a planter of seeds in a garden filled with such beautiful flowers is the responsibility of all queens everywhere.

Basic Black-eyed Peas
Nora Young Turner

1 lb. black-eyed peas
1–2 cups cubed smoked turkey ham
to taste: minced onion, bell pepper, celery, garlic
to taste: salt, black pepper, red pepper, cumin, basil

1. Soak black-eyed peas overnight with enough cold water to completely cover them.
2. Rinse in colander and remove any strange peas or foreign matter.
3. Place peas and enough water to cover them in a 5-quart Dutch oven. Cook all ingredients over low heat in 5-quart Dutch oven until peas are tender (about three to four hours), stirring occasionally.
4. Serve over cooked rice.

Opening Night
Harry Lennix

I got a call from Charlie Jordan, Robert Townsend's capable assistant and a supertalented artist in her own right. Robert, she says, has an idea. A stage version of *The Five Heartbeats*, to be done as a fundraiser for the church that he attends. Would I be interested in coming out to direct it? He's the producer, and the church is putting up the money to refurbish an earthquake-damaged movie house and turning it into a theater. Could I come out? Soon?

You bet I could come out. New York was starting to close in on me. The change might actually be good, for a little while anyway. I made my plans.

When an audience watches a play, if all goes well, all they care about is watching the magic, being engrossed in the story, being entertained. A good team will make the production look easy. Theater excellence ain't easy. Here's a behind-the-scenes look at the trials and tribulations of *The Five Heartbeats*, the stage version.

28 June

After a week in the Windy City, I hit the shaky L.A. ground running. I call the excellent and resourceful Stephanie Scott. I ask humbly if she'll do most of the work everybody else is supposed to do, as usual. She

193

says the only thing she is capable of saying: "Yes." (Hey, I only play with loaded dice.) She helps me assemble:

1 brilliant composer/arranger/musical director (Stephen Taylor)

1 brilliant choreographer/educator (Kenny Long)

1 assistant stage manager (Damont Lamont)

1 remarkable lyricist (Kimberly Blake)

1 knockout set designer (Thom Brown)

1 terrif costumer/seamstress (Ida Muldrow)

2 top-notch film/stage/and television veterans (T'Keyah Kemah and J. J. Jones)

50 wonderful, dedicated, generous, and gifted cast members

Oodles of staff, crew, volunteers, and do-gooders too numerous to name.

14 August

The theater isn't ready. The show is set to open in about two more weeks. Walls need to be taken out. Seats need to be installed. We have to find a band to play accompaniment. There's no way it can all be done in time. I make a note to myself to CALL TOWNSEND.

15 August

The crews will work round the clock. Townsend comforts, no worries.

16 August

Worries.

17 August

Robert and the church leaders decide to push the show back a couple of weeks. Wise decision. This buys me a little needed time, you know, to build a theater from the ground up, using spoons as tools. This, I figure, should take about a week or two.

25 August

Worries. How about pushing the show back another month? "No way," comes the reply. We're already way over budget and behind schedule.

28 August

Hallelujah! The theater is ready.

29 August

The show is not.

30 August

Seven days to the first audience. In all the melee with the physical space getting ready, things have been neglected. Among them are the typical tech-week issues like sound, lighting cues, costume changes, etc. What a mess.

Of course there are some pleasant surprises. Holly Watkins and Christie Douglas emerge as show stoppers. Stephen's songs are nothing but legitimate hits, and Kimberly Blake distinguishes herself as a haunting poet through her lyricism, vocal ability, and performance. Stephen has also solved the band issue by sequencing all the music himself after incalculably long hours in his studio.

But the bad news is that the show is too long. We have to lose some pretty good stuff. My assistant, Nick Gillie, and I also agree that one of the neglected issues is one of the actors. He happens to be in a key role. Unhappily, with all the other stuff that had gone on, he got behind the gun.

This was one of those mea culpas that sneak up on you. We decide to work with him for a couple of days. But time is running out.

2 September

It isn't working out. It becomes apparent that we (well, I) have to replace this extremely nice and talented actor. It simply is not his fault. Had I been more sensitive, it all could have been avoided. But now the show is in this position, and I have to choose between a good person and a good show. In theory, in *principle*, I know exactly what should be done. Choose the principle always. Sounds easy, yet principle doesn't have a heart that can be broken. Principle doesn't look you in the eye when you tell it that it has to be replaced. Principle just is. You can fight for it or fight against it. That's up to the individual and the consequences come to the person choosing. Principle is lucky. It doesn't think it did something wrong when it didn't. It doesn't feel rejected even when it is.

I asked Gillie if I could buy him a chicken-and-waffle breakfast. I needed him to help me make the decisions I had already made—to fire the actor and to call my secret weapon.

The great thing about a secret weapon is that it's secret. You can put it into place and have it ready before, for example, you have to call your producer to tell him you're about to change his whole show around. Fortunately, I had been given a free hand here, and I was working with a producer who trusted me—except I had to secure my weapon first. The call was brief. I have transcribed it verbatim.

"Hello," the voice answered.

"Hey, Dwain?"

"What's up, man? How's it going?"

"Well, not so good. I need you to come out and take over the lead."

"Hasn't the show opened?"

"Nah, you know, it's like a week almost, kinda." I lied without shame. I had a show to pull out of my hat.

Silence. I was all set to hang up the phone to let him chew on it for a while.

"Okay," he said. "I'll be out. Probably tomorrow. I gotta take care of a few things first."

"Okay," I found myself saying. "Call me with the flight info."

I had no time to be impressed or moved or frightened for him or for me, although I was all of those things. I had to call Robert and tell him.

He asked for a rundown. "Can he do it, man? There's not so much time."

"Robert, believe me. He's the best there is."

This was true. Dwain Perry had bailed me out about a hundred times. But I wasn't sure about this time. It was too much to learn. There were songs, dance steps, lines, and blocking to learn. A new city, too. Camaraderie was about to be broken. Relationships had to be constructed in a heartbeat. I had to reassure the cast that this was the best thing for the show.

I had to tell my original actor.

We met for an early breakfast. I had eggs and grits. He had orange juice and a sizable chunk of his heart.

I did a terrible job explaining.

"I can do this job, Harry."

"I believe it, but not under these circumstances. You gotta believe that this is the hardest call I've ever had to make."

"Can you give me one more chance?"

"I've already put in the word."

"Man, oh man." He was crumbling. I felt like crumbs, dirt.

"I'm sorry about this," I said.

"Yeah, me too. *The Five Heartbeats*, together, forever. Wow."

That's how breakfast went. I drove away from there very slowly. When you're two feet tall, it's tough to see over the steering wheel.

Dwain got in that evening. He looked as fresh-faced as a cherub, like he'd lost ten years. I guessed I knew who gained them. I treated him to some chicken and waffles.

"How am I gonna do this?" he asked.

"It's easy. You ain't got time to think about it enough to mess it up." I hoped I was right.

4 September

Perry's first rehearsal. He stumbles through it after having spent the night learning his lines. The morning was spent learning the music. The afternoon learning the steps. He had no script in his hands for the rehearsal.

5 September

Perry walks through it. He has a few flubs. The cast rallies behind him. I see very little of those rehearsals. That night he runs through the show like he was there from the beginning.

6 September

The only thing I'm not worried about is Dwain Perry and the rest of the cast. I don't know how it's possible to have so much heart.

7 September

Hey, this might work out after all—though be clear, the first show was an unmitigated disaster. In fact, I think I'm still watching it. That's how bad the pacing was off. About two light cues (or missed ones as it turned out) into the show, I stopped taking notes. Taking notes in that particular performance was like watching a perfect game being pitched against your team and criticizing your hitters for not running back fast enough to the dugout after being fanned. But with this team there's always a game two. That's the great thing about the theater. You always get a second chance.

I tell you that day, the day of that miserable performance of the *Heartbeats*, was one of the most exciting days of my tenure. As ugly as it was, you could see it taking shape. For intervals of seconds, even minutes, in the midst of the huge technical flubs, there were little snatches of heaven. The funny thing about perfection is that it's like raising a child. To get the thing right takes nurturing, discipline, time, commitment, and of course, love.

We weren't perfect with the show, not ever. But boy, did we get close. On balance, after you factor in the working conditions and lack of dough and a thousand other things, we got damn close. We achieved a level of theater excellence and provided the audience with some excellent theater. I'm not sure you could ask any other church to take such a huge risk on a bunch of people they didn't know (especially when one of the people is me) and build a theater. I don't think you could ask another producer to build a show, literally. I don't think you could ask many other assistants and designers to go the Olympian extremes and lose money to sweat, blood, and acid tears. Certainly, it's hard to ask a guy to learn a three-hour musical in two or three days. And what spirit, what unnameable thing can keep a cast and crew of seventy people of wildly disparate backgrounds and beliefs, for months of uncertainty, for not one red cent? I never figured it out. Sometimes, I think, God doesn't want to be figured out. Sometimes you gotta take a gift for what it is and just say thanks.

Sexual Beatitudes
Gloria Wade-Gayles

"In the worst kind of winds, you have to stand up tall."

My mother was a rose among thorns. Atypical in many ways. She loved privacy, books, and polemics. She was not a "churchified" woman. And she had what, in the forties, was considered a dangerous parenting style, especially for black girls, and more especially those living in a housing project. She did not whip us with thin switches pulled from overgrown bushes. In fact, I did not remember Mama *ever* whipping us, although Grandmama did a few times. She did not arrange our days around a list of household chores, the completion of which took hours. And she gave us too much freedom. Too much latitude. When we had dates, she would greet them, engage them in conversation (sometimes longer than I wanted), and retire for the night. Miss Gotta-Know-and-Then-Tell-Everything was right: we could have gotten pregnant with Mama in the apartment. While she slept upstairs, my sister and I entertained our dates downstairs. Mama's explanation for her atypical behavior: "I trust my girls."

It was, in part, her trust that encouraged my sister and me to follow her sexual beatitudes, and more than once we were convinced that doing so had its rewards, especially when we would walk through rough sections of the neighborhood on our way to work. On hot summer days, men gathered outside a pool hall three doors down from the theater, stripped down to their waists, their biceps glistening in the sun. Judging from their gestures and their raucous laughter, we knew they were telling obscene jokes. When we were within earshot, we would hear, "Man, watch your mouth. Those girls right there? They the Wade Sisters."

With men who did not know us, however, the story was quite different. They would undress us with their eyes and violate us with their words. "Hey, sweet thang," they would call, sometimes touching their genitals suggestively, "I got something for you." Mama and other women advised us against acting offended. If we did, they said, the men would "shonuff talk" about us. One day a friend, who lived in a middle-class community on the other side of town, made the mistake of giving a group of whistling men a disdainful look. The obscenities were like Chinese firecrackers. Bam! Bam! Bam! Staccato explosions! "Who you think wanted you," they began, "with your ugly ass. I'd have to put a bag over your face first, and I still might not want you." Had I been alone, I would have ignored them or smiled and said, as project women advised, "How are you, sir?" It always worked. I swear it always worked. Men would often become so unnerved they would tip an imaginary hat.

The women had different names for men based on their behavior, especially toward women. "Scum" was the category in which they placed men who screamed obscenities at women in public. There were only three categories for young men who dated girls in the project: "lazy," "up to no good," and "decent." More than once I heard the women (but not Miss Gotta-Know-and-Then-Tell-Everything) say to Mama, "Bertha, your girls take up with some decent boys." Our dates *were* "decent boys" who would observe any mother's rules for behavior in her house, but, like the women, they, too, were amazed that Mama was lenient on curfew and did not give them the third degree before we left the apartment. They did not read the smile which said to us, not to them, "I trust you."

I remember the night my date tried to make it down an unpaved road which heavy rains the night before had turned into quicksand. We were pulled into mud that had the hold of a heavy glue. It took a tow truck hours to pull us out. On the way home, my date, wearing the evidence of our experience up to his knees, was afraid that my mother would be angry with him. I was afraid that she was walking the floor in worry.

Before I could turn the key in the lock, the door opened. My mother pulled me toward her in a tight embrace. She had been crying.

"Thank God," she said. "Thank God, you're safe." Not waiting to hear my explanation, she asked, "Are you hungry?"

My mother had walked through the refiner's fire and come out remarkably beautiful in soul. She was a peacemaker. As are most Libras, those who believe in signs would say. To avoid conflict, she made an effort to see the other person's point of view. She was willing to compromise, but not at the sacrifice of her conscience. "That kind of peace is hell," she would say.

She was generous with her money, her love, and her advice.

She was compassionate and especially toward underdogs. She had seen enough in her life to believe that many women suffered because they were women.

"Women can be such pitiful creatures," she would often say. "So dependent. So out of touch with themselves."

It was this philosophy that prevented her from castigating young girls in the community. The only thing girls did not need, in Mama's opinion, was a prediction that they wouldn't amount to any good because females don't. Shore them up. Bolster them. Inject them with pride. "Tell them how wonderful they are."

That was Mama's philosophy, and it translated into her unconditional trust in my sister and me. She believed a mother had to be her daughter's friend and that she should hold back nothing, especially in matters of sex. Which is why in one breath she advised us against premarital sex and in another she discussed sex in a way that could have easily tempted us to do the very thing she said we should not do. She tried to teach us about sexual exploitation, but not at the expense of our sexuality. Mama actually wanted us to *enjoy* sex. But at the right time.

"It's a wonderful experience," she would tell us. "It feels good. And it's beautiful."

If it's all that, I remember saying to myself, why should we deny ourselves?

Mama's explanation made sense. "It's beautiful but not in the back of a car and not in a motel room. It feels good but not when you have to worry about someone finding out."

You can't experience the "real thing," she would tell us, when you have all those worries interfering with your pleasure. "You have to be able to take your time. Take your own good unworried time."

What young boys in heat could take their time? she wondered.

She talked openly about biological differences between women and men and about emotional differences as well. Men could have pleasure in a second, and with anyone. A perfect stranger, in fact. A woman's pleasure, on the other hand, she said, required time, intimacy, and commitment.

"All three are hard to find in a young relationship."

She was not, however, always academic in her sexual teachings. Frequently. Correction. Often, she was pure emotion. Like the other women.

"Just keep this in mind," she would tell us. "That's what a man wants if he can get it."

She taught us how to distinguish between the boys who wanted only that and the others who were genuinely involved with us but would, of course, get it if they could.

She would recite, "If they tell you after the third date that they are madly in love with you. If they can't keep their hands off you. If they rarely want to take you where there are other people. If they say you would do it if you loved them. If they say they don't want to go all the way in. If they threaten to quit you when you continue to say no. If they tell you they are getting sick because they're not getting it. *Leave them alone* because all they want is your body and since that's all they want, once they get it, they're gone.

"And, just think about this," she would add. "If you're having sex with him, how do you know it's you he loves and not the sex?"

In other plain and simple words, sex altered a relationship, and teenagers were far from ready for the alteration.

Another caveat was: "Do not ever touch alcohol. First of all, it's in your family. And second, it robs you of self-control. Don't ever *ever* drink from a cup someone gives you. Only from a bottle, and only from one that *you* opened."

Mama was serious.

And more. "A man does not like a woman who is not a challenge. If you're too easy, he'll lose interest." Was she suggesting that we use denial or our bodies to entrap men? That was *not* what she said. She *said*, don't let men trap us with a lot of jive talk into giving them our bodies before we were ready, before we should. In other words, remain virgins until we married.

Did she say we should save our bodies for a special man? That was *not* what she said because that suggests a man has a deed to a woman's body and a right to her purity. It calls for sexual genuflecting. What she *said* was virginity had nothing at all to do with men and everything to do with women. It gave us protection, self-esteem, and even control.

Was she saying that the desire was in our head and not in our bodies? That was *not* what she said. What a ridiculous idea. What she *said* was, "Of course you are going to want to have sex. That's natural. It's what you're supposed to feel. And if you don't feel it, then something is wrong."

We're supposed to feel something we are not supposed to express? Hmmph. It was easy for her to talk. She was no longer young and in love.

She was not smooching in a car at a drive-in restaurant and dancing a dangerous slow drag on a song that curled your toes the way she said sex can. "Oh, my love, my darling," the voice crooned at a high school dance. "I've hungered for your kiss a long lonely time."

But Mama trusted me, I would tell myself, fighting the urge to give in. The struggle was more difficult in college where many girls, including those who made the Dean's List (which proved that they were not derailed) were sexually active and didn't hide it. Even flaunted it. My knees would buckle when I danced to my favorite song. "Each night before I go to sleep, my baby, I whisper a little prayer for you, my baby." The words were hypnotic, the struggle unbearable. "And tell all the stars above that this is dedicated to the one I love."

She was expecting too much of me. What about the hormones? They had centrifugal power pulling me toward a sexual center.

But Mama trusted us.

What should I do about the centrifugal pull?

She had no easy answers.

She trusted.

"I want you to have it all," she would tell us. "Education. Education. Economic sufficiency. And sexual passion. Pleasure."

Confusion. Struggle. Hormones. Conflict.

But Mama trusted us.

"You'll be glad you waited," she said with certainty that we would wait. "Trust me. You'll be *so* ready. You'll be glad."

Mama was right.

New Directions
Maya Angelou

In 1903 the late Mrs. Annie Johnson of Arkansas found herself with two toddling sons, very little money, a slight ability to read and add simple numbers. To this picture add a disastrous marriage and the burdensome fact that Mrs. Johnson was a Negro.

When she told her husband, Mr. William Johnson, of her dissatisfaction with their marriage, he conceded that he too found it to be less than he expected, and had been secretly hoping to leave and study religion. He added that he thought God was calling him not only to preach but to do so in Enid, Oklahoma. He did not tell her that he knew a minister in Enid with whom he could study and who had a friendly, unmarried daughter. They parted amicably, Annie keeping the one-room house and William taking most of the cash to carry himself to Oklahoma.

Annie, over six feet tall, big-boned, decided that she would not go to work as a domestic and leave her "precious babes" to anyone else's care. There was no possibility of being hired at the town's cotton gin or lumber mill, but maybe there was a way to make the two factories work for her. In her words, "I looked up the road I was going and back the way I come, and since I wasn't satisfied, I decided to step off the road and cut me a new path." She told herself that she wasn't a fancy cook but that she could "mix groceries well enough to scare hungry away and from starving a man."

She made her plans meticulously and in secret. One early evening to see if she was ready, she placed stones in two five-gallon pails and carried them three miles to the cotton gin. She rested a little, and then, discarding some rocks, she walked in the darkness to the sawmill five miles farther along the dirt road. On her way back to her little house and her babies, she dumped the remaining rocks along the path.

That same night she worked into the early hours boiling chicken and frying ham. She made dough and filled the rolled-out pastry with meat. At last she went to sleep.

The next morning she left her house carrying the meat pies, lard, an iron brazier, and coals for a fire. Just before lunch she appeared in an empty lot behind the cotton gin. As the dinner noon bell rang, she dropped the savors into boiling fat and the aroma rose and floated over to the workers who spilled out of the gin, covered with white lint, looking like specters.

Most workers had brought their lunches of pinto beans and biscuits or crackers, onions and cans of sardines, but they were tempted by the hot meat pies which Annie ladled out of the fat. She wrapped them in newspapers, which soaked up the grease, and offered them for sale at a nickel each. Although business was slow those first days, Annie was determined. She balanced her appearances between the two hours of activity.

So, on Monday if she offered hot fresh pies at the cotton gin and sold the remaining cooled-down pies at the lumber mill for three cents, then on Tuesday she went first to the lumber mill presenting fresh, just-cooked pies as the lumbermen covered in sawdust emerged from the mill.

For the next few years, on balmy spring days, blistering summer noons, and cold, wet, and wintry middays, Annie never disappointed her customers, who could count on seeing the tall, brown-skinned woman bent over her brazier, carefully turning the meat pies. When she felt certain that the workers had become dependent on her, she built a stall between the two hives of industry and let the men run to her for their lunchtime provisions.

She had indeed stepped from the road which seemed to have been chosen for her and cut herself a brand-new path. In years that stall became a store where customers could buy cheese, meal, syrup, cookies, candy, writing tablets, pickles, canned goods, fresh fruit, soft drinks, coal, oil, and leather soles for worn-out shoes.

Each of us has the right and the responsibility to assess the roads which lie ahead, and those over which we have traveled, and if the future road looms ominous or unpromising, and the roads back uninviting, then we need to gather our resolve and, carrying only the necessary baggage, step off that road into another direction. If the new choice is also unpalatable, without embarrassment, we must be ready to change that as well.

STEP FIVE

Eating the Peas

Three hours of simmering, and the stew actually smelled like something I might want to eat. It smelled absolutely delicious. I was amazed. I did that? Damn, I'm good!

But as the moment of truth arrived, I got nervous. Suppose the peas were just pretending to smell good? Would they do that to me, after all we'd been through together? That's happened to me before. I was attempting to cook some split pea soup, and the smells of garlic, carrots, and onions were hypnotic. But the taste was bland. I was so disappointed, I threw out the entire batch and boiled some turkey hot dogs instead.

I sat down with my father at the old kitchen table to partake of my creation. I thought about all those great chefs on TV cooking shows when, after having finally completed the dish (in exactly thirty minutes), they sit down, eat, and extol the wonders and magnificence of their work. Well, what else would they say? That sure is some nasty food?

But what if my black-eyed peas dish was a disaster? I hadn't measured not one ingredient. Daddy wouldn't let me. Every herb, every spice, every bean and vegetable that went in the pot was selected based on my fledgling intuitive powers. I poured salt in my cupped hand instead of measuring with a teaspoon— Daddy swore that the cupped palm never failed to measure a teaspoon. But what if my hand was smaller than his? Didn't matter. Once, I saw a TV chef make a similar claim. He poured some herb in his hand, then let it slip into a teaspoon. It was exactly right!

"You ready?" Daddy asked me. Out of courtesy and old-fashioned (but nice) southern gentlemanliness, he waited for me to eat first. I nodded, looking down at the bowl. It did look and smell delicious, like a Louis Armstrong tune—hot, smoky, and happy. I closed my eyes and said a silent prayer. *God is great. God is good. Please be merciful to this food, Amen.*

I scooped a pile of rice and plopped it on my plate. I ladled a generous helping of the peas dish on top. Gingerly, prayerfully, I took my first taste. I let the different flavors play and dance on my tongue.

My mouth was happy. My lips curled into a smile. Daddy looked at me and grinned. "Lord, that's some good mess!" I said.

Our apprentice and her teacher eat reverently. The black-eyed peas dish is a great success. She's learned that excellence in cooking is as much an art as it is a science. With all her senses she searches for each individual spice, herb, and vegetable. The grittiness of the peas against her tongue reminds her of a man's caress or her son's woolly head. It's a sensuous dish that makes her think of cotton fields and hot sun and overcoming adversity. She imagines Martin Luther King, Fannie Lou Hamer, and maybe even Malcolm X eating black-eyed peas after a hot march or during a stint in some dusty jail cell.

A Remedy for Racism
Dick Gregory

Good evening, ladies and gentlemen. I understand there are a good many Southerners in the room tonight. I know the South very well. I spent twenty years there one night. . . .

It's dangerous for me to go back. You see, when I drink, I think I'm Polish. One night I got so drunk I moved out of my own neighborhood. . . .

Last time I was down South I walked into this restaurant, and this white waitress came up to me and said: "We don't serve colored people here."

I said: "That's all right, I don't eat colored people. Bring me a whole fried chicken."

About that time these three cousins come in, you know the ones I mean, Klu, Kluck, and Klan, and they say: "Boy, we're givin' you fair warnin'. Anything you do to that chicken, we're gonna do to you." About then the waitress brought me my chicken. "Remember, boy, anything you do to that chicken, we're gonna do to you." So I put down my knife and fork, and I picked up that chicken, and I *kissed* it.

Lessons in Joy from the Bionic Woman

Ruth Beckford

One of my missions in life is to spread the good word about positive thinking and living a joyful life. All during my life as a dancer and in my second career as an actress, I have made it my business to help raise people's spirits and their self-worth. I was a motivational speaker way before it became fashionable. I believe there's just no reason to go through life moping around. Like I tell all my friends, especially young people, try new things! Believe in yourself. There are too many good things to enjoy. Regardless of economic circumstances, age, race, or looks you can decide to be happy; it's all about how you perceive your circumstances. One person looks at a lemon and his mouth puckers up; another sees sweet lemonade.

So imagine my surprise when, for the first time in my life at sixty-three years of age, I experienced that clinical condition that is commonly called depression. I had just had my third of four back surgeries back in 1989 when a wave of sorrow hit me, and hard. Now I understand that many people who experience depression get used to the feeling and learn to live with it, but for me, this was completely new, and I didn't know what to do about it. I didn't like it. It didn't feel good at all.

Intellectually I knew why I was depressed: here I was, an independent, capable woman reduced to having to depend on others for the first time in her life. It was hard for me to accept having someone to come and do things for me. I'm always the helper. I couldn't even turn my own body by myself. A nurse had to come and help me, I was in so much pain.

Before I was released from the hospital I told the doctor that I wanted to talk to a shrink. I believe in talking to shrinks. She told me that I was depressed because I was in great pain and I feared another back surgery. She also told me what I already knew, that I hated being dependent on anyone. My case is so bad that before I went into the hospital, I baked a turkey, sliced it, and bagged many single meals knowing that I would have a long hospital stay and home convalescence. I didn't want my sister and my friends taking time away from their families to cook for me.

I went home in a walker—me, a dancer, dependent on a mechanical thing to help me walk. I would start crying for no reason at all. Somebody would say, "Hi, how are you doing?" and I'd say, "Waa waa waa." Turn on the TV, and I would start boohooing.

"This is not me," my mind would say over and over, but my heart and spirit were slow to catch up.

After a while, the depression lifted, but it did not go away by itself. I had to work hard at reclaiming my joy. Here's some things to think about doing to help you bounce back from trials and tribulations.

1. Feed your mind with positive thoughts. Listen to upbeat tapes and read inspirational books. Read them upon awakening and before you go to bed.
2. Affirm your highest good always. Even when things look bleak, know, without a shadow of a doubt, that life will get better.
3. Make yourself laugh. Norman Cousins healed himself by watching old-time comedy movies. Laughter is a healing force for body and soul. Depression has a hard time thriving in a body that's al-

ways laughing. (I also love to read trashy novels. They have the same effect on me.)

4. Be flexible. A resilient spirit is made when you leave yourself room to make mistakes and change plans.

5. When all else fails, pray the following prayer: *I let go and let God work his magic.*

A Funny Thing Happened on the Way to the Hospital

Stephanie J. Gates

I am living proof that when God wrote the script for my life, he had a good sense of humor. My trials and tribulations have often taken on a comical twist. I have laughed until I cried, and cried until I laughed. Laughter is sometimes the only thing that will get us through the pain.

The first time I experienced back pain was in December of 1986. I bent over to get something out of the refrigerator, and I was literally stuck in that position. So, off I went to the emergency room, walking like the Hunchback of Notre Dame minus the hump.

The doctor twisted my legs into various pretzel positions, then they rolled me into X ray. The diagnosis: sprained/strained lumbar. I was sent home with some painkillers and spent the next four weeks on my back.

All was well up until the spring of 1987. I had gone to see a chiropractor, and his manipulations seemed to help. Feeling confident that I was ready to move, I went to the health club to get my sweat on. I made a wrong move in an aerobics class and felt something pop in my lower back.

I returned to the chiropractor for one treatment, but did not follow his advice to come back at least one more time. I felt fine. But oh, how I learned the hard way that a hard head makes a hurt back.

That weekend, I was scheduled to take some of my nieces, nephews, and another friend to the movies. My back was throbbing, and I really didn't want to go, but I had promised to take them to the show.

We had to take the bus, and it was raining. When the bus came, I swung Billy up on the bus trying to avoid a puddle. I forgot to bend my knees. Small move, big mistake. Billy was a much heavier three-year-old than I had anticipated. A good-sized tree branch snapped in half in my back, and the gremlins of pain emerged and diligently began to work.

By the time we got to the show, the gremlins were working overtime. Unable to sit, I slouched down in the chair, trying to take the pressure off my back. After the movie, I dropped Khalilah off, took Billy home, and waited there for one of my sisters to pick us up. The Cosby Kids were turning into Bebe's Kids, and I had to get them back to their parents.

When I got home I just lay on my back with my knees bent. It was the only position that provided some relief. Every so often a gremlin would plant a stick of dynamite in my back and light the fuse. I rolled back and forth to extinguish the pain. I refused to go to the emergency room. I wanted to wait until Monday when I could get in to see one of the doctors at Mary Thompson Hospital (MTH) where I worked. I thought I could get better care there than in some emergency room. You live and learn.

By Monday, my back was barely supporting my body weight. The pain was shooting down my left leg. I felt weak, and everything seemed to be moving in s-l-o-w motion. The events that followed are true. My trip to the hospital played out like a script for a Leslie Nielsen emergency room movie spoof. It began when my sister, Debra, came home to take me to MTH. I had already called to let them know I'd be coming.

Debra will be the first to admit that even though she means well and tries to be helpful, she is not good at handling emergencies. While I was getting myself ready to go to the hospital, my mother went to McDonald's to get lunch for my nephew Marcus. When Debra went into the kitchen and left me in the den, the room began dancing, and I didn't think I could keep up. "Debra, I think I'm about to fall out," I called out to her. She came back into the room, handed me the broom, and said, "Here, hold on to this." She went back into the kitchen, and I did as I was told. Then it was lights out on the dance floor. "Deeebraaaahhh!"

When Debra walked back into the room, I was about to pass out. My eyes rolled up in my head, and I reached for her. She moved. (I didn't know this until I heard her telling someone the story. I thought I had passed out before she came back into the room.) Debra said when she saw the whites of my eyes, she thought I had died.

Forgetting about Marcus, Debra flew out of the house and ran out into the street yelling for help. My mother was on her way back, and when she saw Debra, she jumped out of the car. "Stephanie, Stephanie" was all Debra could gasp. She didn't know how to tell my mother I had died. Momma ran up the stairs and saw Marcus standing over me saying, "Wake up, Tee-Tee." I looked up into the faces of Momma, Debra, and Marcus and couldn't figure out how I had ended up on my back without dying from the pain.

Debra decided to call Luke, a guy we know who drinks liquor like kids eat candy. He rushed right over with a friend. They decided to carry me out on the ironing board.

They lifted me up onto the ironing board and proceeded to carry me from the second floor down the winding stairs to the car. They laid me on my side with my knees bent, and I was clutching the ironing board with both hands. I just knew they were going to drop me and it showed on my face.

"What's wrong with you?" Momma asked as she looked into my wide, wild eyes.

"I'm scared they're going to drop me," I whispered, but thankfully, the ride was smooth. Not a bump or a thump.

When we arrived at the hospital, two of the transporters came first with a wheelchair, then a gurney. Gently, they lifted me and placed me on the gurney, but in their haste to get me into the emergency room, they rammed the gurney into the door. Leslie Nielsen was surely laughing in the wings somewhere.

I've worked at MTH since I was seventeen, and so I've gotten to know many of the employees. Nurse Basilgo, in particular, was a very sweet person, but a little high-strung and impatient sometimes. I've always told my coworkers that if I was ever sick to please don't let Nurse Basilgo be on duty in the emergency room.

Of course she was on duty when I arrived. Before any X rays could be taken I had to take a pregnancy test (standard procedure). Since I couldn't walk to the bathroom, I had to use a bedpan to give a urine sample. I guess it was taking me too long to get the pan underneath me, so Basilgo just grabbed it and rammed it under me. Never mind that there was a mine in my back just waiting to blow up. It did, but somehow I managed to give her a urine sample.

Basilgo sent my urine to the lab, but she forgot to put a stat sticker on it so it could be analyzed immediately. My urine sat in the lab for forty-five minutes, and I lay there in pain the entire time. The shift changed, and God, who must have sent an angel in training to watch over me that day, *finally* sent reinforcements in the name of Betty Parks. Betty was the best nurse's assistant who ever walked the planet. She should have been an RN or a doctor. In less than fifteen minutes, she had the results of my test. Negative. On to X ray.

I kept up an inner dialog; I told myself that it would all be over soon. It simply could not get any worse. My back had been jarred twice and the doctor had not even touched me. Bobby, the Radiology supervisor, and Isaac, the technician, were both going to take my X rays since I was practically immobile. They decided to lift me on the count of three.

Remember that routine that Danny Glover and Mel Gibson did in *Lethal Weapon II?* One of them lifted on three, and the other one lifted on four. On the count of three, half my body went up, and the other half stayed on the gurney. And just like in the movie, they argued about whose fault it was. I rolled over on the table as the tears rolled down my cheeks.

The X ray was negative and all my blood tests were normal. Dr. Duret speculated that perhaps I blacked out because I had surpassed my threshold for pain. He wanted to transfer me to another hospital to get a CAT scan. Here I was, the star of my own movie and doing my own stunts. I just knew this movie was going to end on a high note. But nothing is ever over until it's over. I began to relax because the only thing left for me to do was get a pain shot. As soon as the medicine kicked in, I was on my way to Mount Sinai.

There was a new nurse on duty. I can't remember her name, but I'll always remember how she stabbed me in my hip with that needle like she was trying to cut a tough steak. I jumped, which, of course, jarred my back. Oh, the pain. The credits rolled as I awaited the ambulance to take me away.

Nine days in Mount Sinai Hospital revealed a herniated disc and possibly a pinched nerve. I walked out of the hospital wearing a steel girdle that I now keep as a souvenir.

I work out four to five times a week, and if I'm careful about how I lift objects, pay attention to early warning signs, and see the chiropractor for a maintenance checkup, I live relatively pain free.

The most important lesson I learned from my comedy of errors was that anything that I can laugh at, I can live with.

Finding the Proper Joy
Bertice Berry

When I got my Ph.D., I gave thanks to God and knew that I should celebrate. (By the way, isn't it strange that after his acquittal for the murders of Ron Goldman and Nicole Brown Simpson, O. J. Simpson didn't go running into the nearest church to thank God—any God?) Anyway, I wanted to do something that would commemorate my achievement and reward me for my hard work.

Initially I had promised myself the reward of one-carat diamond earrings. I'd read that certain tribes in Africa would pierce their ears only after they had done something of major significance. I knew that in the eighteenth century sailors pierced an ear only after they had sailed around the world or survived a significant shipwreck. My achievement was pretty clear. Getting a Ph.D. was like surviving a shipwreck.

I had pierced my right ear when I'd passed my comprehensive exams, another tough journey. Now I was eager to pierce my left ear so that people would stop asking me stupid questions like, "What does it mean to have only one earring? Are you gay or something?"

But then I recalled reading about the horrible conditions in the diamond mines in South Africa—the work was full of danger for its barely paid work. And I knew that most of the diamonds imported by the United States came from South Africa, which still operated under apartheid. Was this something I wanted to be reminded of every time I thought about my Ph.D.?

In thinking about my reward to myself, I was also challenged by something Alice Walker had written. She said, "If we value that which is plentiful over that which is scarce, then the revolution can take place." I decided that I didn't need diamond earrings after all, that I would rather put shells in my ears than diamonds. And that's what I did. Now whenever I put those earrings on, they mean something; they are symbols of all that I value, love, and respect. They remind me of the qualities that I know God wants me to feel in myself. And they remind me that the revolution is coming.

Once when I was on the comedy road, driving through the Florida panhandle, for one reason or another I was doubting myself and my work. During this doubt session, I was listening to Bob Marley's "Try Jah Love."

I began to pray and to ask God what my true purpose was. In the past, I had frequently asked God what to do in any given circumstance, but I hadn't given extensive thought to my overall purpose in life. Dr. Na'im Akbar, a Black psychologist, talks about the need to ask yourself, Why am I here now? I began to meditate on this question. I got my answer. God instructed me to be happy.

I thought this was the devil speaking, so I prayed again.

God said, "Yo, it's me. I want you to be happy and to share that happiness with others."

Always one for a good debate, I then asked, So, what is sin?

In reply God said, "That which makes you unhappy."

This idea was startling in its simplicity, but I deeply felt its truth. It's amazing how some of the most complicated things are really quite simple—like math.

I started thinking about the best relationships between parents and their children, the kind where parents want to see their child happy and will do almost anything to make it so. But these parents also know that for their child to be happy, there are things the child must avoid, so the parents protect the child for as long as possible. Eventually the child must begin to experience things for himself. So the parent says, "Don't do this, don't do that," and the child asks, "Why?" And the parents say, "Because it's not good for you. It will make you unhappy."

Once when I shared this view with a friend, he accused me of being a hedonist. I pointed out that I worked far too hard to say that pleasure was my only goal, but that I also did not want to be trapped in a world of do's and don'ts.

I've always wanted to try and live and operate within God's perfect plan for my life, but it was only as I got older that I realized God's will is not as rigid as I had thought. There are countless ways to work within this plan, countless choices that will enable me to service Her will and my happiness at the same time.

I've discovered that what makes me happy is entertaining and educating at the same time. The way I go about this has already changed several times, and I'll probably find many other variations before I'm done. But because I feel God's blessing every time I work to fulfill my purpose, and because I believe that everything in my life up to this point has prepared me for it, I have no doubt that I have found the path God hoped I would follow.

Peace.

Happy Birthday To Me!
John Turk

I'm a musician, been playing for a lot of years, but the one gig that stands out in my mind was the one I did last night. It was special because my daughter, kids (John III and Sophia), grandkids, church members, senior citizens that I play for, and entertainment buddies were all there. The place was full, everybody was smiling, everybody was having a good time. Me, my band, and some singers, we played for the crowd. I played a lot of blues, like "Sweet Little Angel." It was just great to be around family and friends who really like you. They weren't there for the flash. They made me feel liked, loved, warm.

The best gig of my life was a surprise birthday party that I threw for myself, and I was surprised at how many people showed up—a couple hundred. We were in a real small place, it only holds about 75, so the joint was packed. Some people had to sit outside. There was no dancing or anything, just my music and people listening to it. I was fortunate to have some great musicians playing with me, and we jammed all night long. To play for friends and family only, that was the most satisfying thing. Why? Because your friends know you.

Fans only know musicians through their music. But to know me as a person, to know that I actually have kids, that I have a life off the stage,

225

that I'm not just some cat playing the clubs or directing the church choir. That's what was important to me.

So last night, I played the trumpet and the piano and I sang for my family and friends. My kids sang the Happy Birthday song to me while I played. I played it straight—no jazz or blues—and it was wonderful. Just to see everybody smiling like that, *man.*

There's nothing like playing music, nothing in the world because I'm talking to you and you're understanding what I'm saying but I'm not saying any words. For me to be able to communicate with you without touching you, to make you feel either good or sad or happy, it's better than making love. If you're playing a love song, people *feel* the love. It can't get much better than that.

A band is just like a basketball team. Everybody has a role to play. When you're on, you can tell because the people respond to you. Sometimes you might think that you didn't do that well, but somebody will come up to you and say, "Man, you were smokin'." And I was about ready to give people their money back. That's because you're always critical of yourself. You hope what you're doing is working, but it doesn't always work. I always try to be at least good, but there are nights when you are excellent, and you don't know when those nights are going to happen. You don't know when, like they say in church, the spirit is going to fill you. You can't bottle it, you can't make it happen. But when it does, you can feel it when you get that thang. Michael Jordan says he goes into another zone. You know when you're there, and you don't know how you got there, but you know you're there.

That's what keeps me going and that's what keeps me playing. I'm just supposed to play, I guess. Thirty years of playing music and I've actually been able to make a living. Raise kids. Buy a home. Buy a couple of new cars. So last night was a celebration of not only my life and the love that's in it, but my music. My music, my life, I guess it's the same thing, and I'm glad I didn't miss the party.

A Well Earned Joy
Frederick Douglass

I found employment, the third day after my arrival, in stowing a sloop with a load of oil. It was new, dirty, and hard work for me; but I went at it with a glad heart and a willing hand. I was now my own master. It was a happy moment, the rapture of which can be understood only by those who have been slaves. It was the first work, the reward of which was to be entirely my own. There was no Master Hugh standing ready, the moment I earned the money, to rob me of it. I worked that day with a pleasure I had never before experienced. I was at work for myself and newly-married wife. It was to me the starting-point of a new existence. When I got through with that job, I went in pursuit of a job of calking; but such was the strength of prejudice against color, among the white calkers, that they refused to work with me, and of course I could get no employment. Finding my trade of no immediate benefit, I threw off my calking habiliments, and prepared myself to do any kind of work I could get to do. Mr. Johnson kindly let me have his wood-horse and saw, and I very soon found myself a plenty of work. There was no work too hard— none too dirty. I was ready to saw wood, shovel coal, carry wood, sweep the chimney, or roll oil casks,—all of which I did for nearly three years in New Bedford, before I became known to the anti-slavery world.

In about four months after I went to New Bedford, there came a young man to me, and inquired if I did not wish to take the "Liberator." I told him I did; but, just having made my escape from slavery, I remarked that I was unable to pay for it then. I, however, finally became a subscriber to it. The paper came, and I read it from week to week with such feelings as it would be quite idle for me to attempt to describe. The paper became my meat and my drink. My soul was set all on fire. Its sympathy for my brethren in bonds—its scathing denunciations of slaveholders—its faithful exposures of slavery—and its powerful attacks upon the upholders of the institution—sent a thrill of joy through my soul, such as I had never felt before!

I had not long been a reader of the "Liberator," before I got a pretty correct idea of the principles, measures and spirit of the anti-slavery reform. I took right hold of the cause. I could do but little; but what I could, I did with a joyful heart, and never felt happier than when in an anti-slavery meeting. I seldom had much to say at the meetings, because what I wanted to say was said so much better by others. But, while attending an anti-slavery convention at Nantucket, on the 11th of August, 1841, I felt strongly moved to speak, and was at the same time much urged to do so by Mr. William C. Coffin, a gentleman who had heard me speak in the colored people's meeting at New Bedford. It was a severe cross, and I took it up reluctantly. The truth was, I felt myself a slave, and the idea of speaking to white people weighed me down. I spoke but a few moments, when I felt a degree of freedom, and said what I desired with considerable ease. From that time until now, I have been engaged in pleading the cause of my brethren—with what success, and with what devotion, I leave those acquainted with my labors to decide.

Creating Joy
Sarah and Bessie Delany

The Delany sisters, Sarah and Bessie, are bestselling centenarians. Their critically acclaimed memoir, *Having Our Say: The Delany Sisters' First 100 Years* had a twenty-eight-week run on *The New York Times* bestseller list. As Bessie used to say, "Not bad for two old inky-dinks over one hundred years old!"

Bessie: I'd say one of the most important qualities to have is the ability to create joy in your life. Of course, at my age, it's a joy even to be breathing! Sometimes I joke with Sadie, "I sure am lucky that I'm so good at the things I enjoy the most—eating, sleeping, and talking!"

But when I was younger, I found joy in so many different things. My friends and neighbors. My church. And I dearly loved my flowers and vegetables. We filled our yard with them: wild plum trees, pear trees, fig trees, grapes, blackberries, raspberries, strawberries, African onions, leeks, corn, string beans, okra, squash, cauliflower, cabbage, tomatoes, and rhubarb.

There's nothing like a garden to help you appreciate the passage of time. In the spring, when those brave little crocuses and snowdrops poke up, we cheer them on. Then in March or early April come the daffodils. Then the tulips, and so on, until all the flowers bloom at once: lily of the valley, phlox, black-eyed Susan, cosmos, daisies, and, of course, roses. For some reason, we were always partial to red roses, so we planted more of those.

We never stopped improving our garden. Anytime someone gave us cut flowers as a gift, we would save the seeds and plant them in the spring. Here's a secret: If you're pressed for time, just drop dead flowers on the ground in your garden. The leaves and stems will become mulch and often the seeds will "take" by themselves. There's no need to ever throw out old cut flowers.

The plants I love most are the ones that come from little clippings we brought back years ago from down South. We'd just take a little snip and bring it back and root it. Why, we have a piece of our grandma's rose of Sharon growing right next to our front steps and some of her bridal wreath, too. And we have daylilies and iris lilies from the property of Mrs. Hunter, the wife of the principal at Saint Aug's when we were children. Having those plants is like having our homefolks here with us!

I love my garden so much that I would stay out there all day long if Sadie let me. That's what I mean by creating joy in your life. We all have to do it for ourselves.

Sadie: You know, my life has been filled with joy, too. My joy is Bessie.

The Summer the Father Became a Mother

Ralph Cheo Thurmon

DADDY'S MAYBE

"Waaaa, waaa!"

Babies' laments were the sounds of my summer.

I operated an illegal day care center. The little criminals were my four small children, tall on mischief and mayhem. Names and ages are unimportant. They were preadolescent and I was a postpartum father. I was incarcerated for the summer. Immobility was my electric chair. Guilty on all accounts of being a father.

How can children be so mischievous? Jeff Fort and Al Capone couldn't have proven more treacherous than my children. All summer long they tap-danced upon edges of my nervous system.

Where are mothers when fathers need them? The mothers of these four children were working. Off for the summer, I was the likely candidate for baby-sitting. September stretched before me, with its promise of satisfying work as a creative writing consultant and youth development professional, teaching, socializing, and culturizing other children across the United States. Well, at least I could spend time with my own for the summer. This was the rationale.

I survived the first week victoriously, so I thought, with no casualties and just a few minor injuries. That weekend, instead of performing my poetry at the African Arts Festival, I nursed a juice-bottle-busted head and a scratched cornea, and retrieved bananas from up the nose. I nursed a summer cold that came from four mucous-dripping little demons whose ancestors come from Africa. Daddy's maybe? Well!

MAMAS' BABIES

Saturday afternoon I sat before the babies' council of elders: three mothers. The mother of my oldest college-bound son scrutinized my first week, and she wasn't impressed.

"Had a rough time your first week, huh, Baba Olu?" Mother said. Names are unimportant. Mothers are all mothers, and these three stared at me intensely.

"No, I was in control from day one," I said, fully aware that African fatherhood was at stake.

"The two toddlers have diaper rash," Mother continued.

"You have to change them on schedule," said another.

"Peanut butter and jelly is not something children should eat every day and all day."

"The walls are not Crayola canvases."

"The couch pillows are torn apart."

"The carpet may have to be replaced. Drool is the worst stain."

"The VCR, CD player, TV, and radio must all be taken to the repair shop."

John Coltrane's cosmic music played in my aching, elephant-sized head. I took each blow to the lower extremities like Ali took Frazier's left hook to the jaw. Like a man. I fell and stood up in one motion. Most people agree Ali should have stayed down longer. Like Ali, I said nothing. What could Father say when his manhood, like Ali's jaw, was broken?

The mothers conferenced among themselves as I sat before them in the father-zone. Continually, they used the word "experiment." Experiment? Was I a summer experiment? Who were the guinea pigs? Who were the scientists? Me or the children?

ADVENTURE AT NAVY PIER

"Where is Ife? Ifeee!" Ife is my three-year-old.

"There's a little girl in the lake!" screamed a bearded man, pointing his walking stick at Lake Michigan.

I rose like Robo-Cop, stepped away from my untouched tossed salad, and looked into the eyes of Abike, my six-year-old for a millisecond. It was her assignment to watch Ife while I focused on the twins, Abiodun and Awodola, who were twenty months.

"Abike, where is FeFe?" I shouted as I ran. Abike sat looking like Mantan Moreland.

I ran to jump in Lake Michigan. I knocked down ten people. At the stone-bank of the lake, a blue-eyed woman with scalelike skin held me by my wrist.

"Look," she pointed. "The child is swimming. Come, dear." She reached her arms out, pulled Ife to her bosom.

I looked stupid, like I'd just heard a James Brown lyric.

"What a great father you are," the woman told me. "I told my lazy son-in-law just this morning that every father should teach his babies how to swim." Not only had I not taught Ife to swim, but I'd drown in dishwater.

"Thank you kindly, ma'am," I said.

She handed Ife to me. I smacked her to my chest like a wet platypus catfish. She grinned and chuckled and the world was back in focus.

When Ife and I reached the outdoor cafe, Dun and Dola were red with catsup and fries. Abike was gone. Her cup of lemonade stood half emptied on the table. I did not crumble like a cracker. I was wet. I sort of wafted like a cookie in milk.

With Dun and Dola in arm and Ife marking our trail with wet tracks, we set out to find Abike. Once again, many eyes were upon us.

There is nothing scarier to a parent than when a child is lost in a crowd of thousands of people. Every horror crossed my mind, every prayer mumbled from my mouth. I am neither Christian nor Muslim, but if Jesus and Allah could bring my baby back, I'd shout Amen and as-salaam-alaikum. I prayed in tongues, many different tongues.

We walked the two-mile Navy Pier dock with a trail of security officers, policemen, and a host of caring people who had joined the crusade to find Abike.

Tears exploded from my eyes that were itching from summer allergy. I went into hysterics, screaming, "Abike is big sister and she knows better." I felt like I was out at sea, overboard without a life jacket. The council of mothers would have my head. How could Abike watch Ife when she can't watch herself? they'd say. I love my children. I had been loving them all summer. More intensely now. Now I knew what it felt like to love them, not as a father, but as a mother.

A crowd of almost 100 people cried and prayed for Abike. They surrounded me as if I were in a womb. My water broke and I cried and cried. It had been one hour.

"Baby Orishamola, come to the information desk," the loudspeaker exclaimed in a demanding voice. I didn't know if I had miscarried and would never see Abike alive again. I would give my life for my daughter, as mothers do bit by sacrificial bit every time they birth a baby.

The children, my sympathetic and empathetic cohorts, and me, climbed the two flights of concrete steps. At the top, standing next to the information desk, flanked by the biggest Ferris wheel in all the world, was the most missed child in history, my Abike.

She ran to me and clutched me, limp as a rag doll. She had been just as worried as we'd been. Before I could speak, she began wiping the tears from my face with the yellow flower on her buba.

"Baba Olu, I was trying to find the water. You told me to watch FeFe," Abike said.

The tears on her face flowed into the tears of the father who, for the summer, had become a mother.

Making People Laugh

Morrie Turner

A cartoonist is not necessarily an artist. He can be. I feel that I'm both. A cartoonist, unlike an artist, is also a writer. He looks at society and writes about it. While he's writing about it he tries to be funny. If he can teach, he does that, too.

One of my favorite Black cartoonists was Samuel Maili. He did a strip on Negro history. Every week I'd clip it. Not only was he a great artist, but the information was mind-blowing. I used to make little scrapbooks of his stuff. I also liked "Bootsy" by Oliver Harrington. I used to rave about his work. Someone from the National Cartoon Society recently told me that he had just been found. "What do you mean he was just found?" I asked. Well, apparently, he had left America, like so many Black writers during the Harlem Renaissance, gone to France, and found work there. He was sent to East Germany on an assignment, got caught, and didn't get back until the Berlin Wall came down.

I was the first syndicated cartoonist to use a Black character. I had no idea that I was going to be a cartoonist. I enjoyed cartoons and I used to draw them all the time, but I did not make any attempt to do anything serious until I got into the service. There I found out that by drawing for the newspapers, I could get out of doing marching drills.

"Wee Pals" by Morrie Turner

STEP SIX

Napping

Following the meal that she has made with her own two hands, our heroine and her father retire to the living room. There the television broadcasts a lively game of football. She knows that watching the game is part of the Sunday ritual, and she'd love to continue bonding with her father in this way, but she simply cannot hang. The old sleep spirit of the living room possesses her body and she cannot resist its seductive charms. She sinks deeply into the sofa, her tummy full and satisfied, and the sleep spirit transports her to the land of dreams. If she can cook a decent pot of black-eyed peas, then anything is possible! Miracles can still come true! Her last sight before succumbing to slumber is of a brother who has made a touchdown. He is dancing and slam-dunking the ball, and mercy, does he look good in those tight spandex pants. . . .

A Way Out of No Way
Andrew Young

God can still "make a way out of no way."

This affirmation has become real to us as a family in the past few years. Our trust in God has almost always had a social or political focus. Our personal faith was tested in the course of our efforts to engage in the social aspects of the gospel, and while this required a tremendous amount of personal prayer and soul searching, there was always the idea that what we were doing was a matter of our own choosing to interpret the will of God in a particular manner. Technically, we could have chosen another form of ministry or a different kind of challenge. But on July 26, 1991, all that changed. We were confronted with a deeply personal challenge from which there was no escape.

After three wonderful weeks together on a business trip to Zimbabwe followed by a weekend in the Bahamas with all our children, their spouses, and our grandchildren, Jean was awakened at home by severe stomach pains. Normally we would have attributed this to the strain of travel and the excesses of food and family in the heat of the Bahamas. But since we had been in Africa, there was the possibility of some strange virus or parasite disturbing her digestion, so I insisted on going to the emergency room at Crawford Long Hospital to get Jean checked out before I went to work.

Jean had never been ill. She had natural childbirth with each of four children and spent only a couple of days in the hospital with each. Serious illness was beyond our comprehension. You can imagine the shock when the doctor told me that there was a tumor blocking her intestine and that an emergency operation was necessary. He also added that in his years of experience such tumors were almost always malignant.

I was still hopeful as she went into surgery. We had been together almost forty years. Jean was really the backbone of our family. There was no way we could conceive of life without her vivacious, energetic spirit. But after the operation, the surgeon informed me that there was an indication that the malignancy had spread to her liver. He was very sensitive to our situation but suggested that chemotherapy might slow the spread of the cancer. He explained that the risk and success rate of chemotherapy and surgery were such that we should make the most of the time that we had left and make life as meaningful as possible for the next few months. Jean should have at least six months and possibly as much as a year to live with colon cancer that had metastasized to the liver. I was numb.

Jean was still in intensive care as I received this message. I walked almost entranced by the horror of this announcement, and I passed the little chapel in the hospital. I entered and fell to my knees at the altar and finally let go of the tears that had welled up in me as a result of the most intense strain of my life. I had been somewhat prepared for Martin's death. He never let us forget what was at stake. I was even very philosophical about the possibility of my own death. I had been happy and surprised to turn fifty, but I could not live without Jean. Her leaving us was a tragedy that no one could consider.

As I ran out of tears and dried my eyes, I looked down at the open Bible on the altar and began to read Psalm 103.

Bless the Lord, O my soul;
And all that is within me, bless His holy name!
Bless the Lord, O my soul,
And forget not all His benefits:
Who forgives all your iniquities,
Who heals all your diseases.

(vv. 1–3)

It was as though each word of this familiar psalm leaped off the page and into my heart. As is the case for most of us, we are lured by the hymns and anthems which emphasize, "Bless the Lord, O my soul," but until we are really confronted with a life-threatening illness, we don't pay much attention to the affirmation "He forgives all our sins, and He heals all our diseases." Now, my concern was the healing of Jean's cancer.

I remembered my experiences with Mrs. Hadley and her cancer years before in Beachton, Georgia. She was given a few months to live and lived at least thirty years longer and died in her late eighties. I wasn't sure what the prescription was, but one thing seemed clear: we must all be determined as a family to win this battle.

There was some evidence in heart attack victims that those who were well-loved had a much better recovery rate than those who had problem relationships or who were in need of love and affection. Also, we were too highly visible in Atlanta to keep secret such a serious crisis. Our friends responded immediately, and several churches across the community remembered us in their prayers. Even the newspapers respected our desire not to have any publicity, but the word spread nevertheless. We soon realized that we were surrounded by an extremely loving and supportive city. A family at prayer that is supported by a loving community is a powerful healing force, especially when backed up by good medicine and a network of nutritional and herbal approaches to the disease. Jean took charge of her own healing with the able assistance of some of the world's best oncologists and surgeons. But it was her life to live, and she didn't just sit back and do as she was told. She began to listen to her own body and use her own mind and the power of her spirit to direct her recovery.

A life-threatening illness forced us to a new level of religious sensitivity and awareness. Perhaps we and others should find ways to always be so sensitive to the spiritual realities, but nothing dominates one's attention like a doctor's death sentence. We've learned that once anyone begins to pay attention to the healing powers of faith and medicine, he or she is on the way to wholeness.

The church as a healing community comes to bear on an illness in an amazing way. As people heard of our situation we received wonderful letters and cards of encouragement, but also tracts and literature on health and healing, and finally two phone calls from dear friends from both coasts. Dr. John Maguire, chancellor of Claremont University in California, put us in touch with one of the best surgeons on the West Coast. Dr. Levi Watkins, associate dean of surgery at Johns Hopkins Medical Center, offered to pull a team of Johns Hopkins specialists together to offer an evaluation of Jean's medical condition. As a youth in Montgomery, Alabama, Levi had been a member of Dexter Avenue Baptist church and had assisted Martin and the Montgomery Improvement Association by helping to clean the cars in the car pool. We accepted the offer from Levi and Johns Hopkins because it was closer geographically and because Andrea and Paula were living in Washington, D.C., only forty miles from the hospital. The result of the evaluation offered the first real medical hope that we had received.

Dr. James Sitzmann of Johns Hopkins, who had specialized in liver surgery, thought that Jean's cancer was operable if it had not spread beyond the liver. He suggested six months of general chemotherapy to curtail the spread of the disease. If after six months there was no indication of the disease spreading, he thought he could operate and remove the tumors from her liver.

At times I thought that the chemotherapy was worse than the disease. I still think that there is something terribly primitive about the approach of chemotherapy, but for now I thank God for it and Dr. Douglas Collins who administered it. Jean also became a vegetarian, drank Chinese herb teas, and developed a pattern of prayer and meditation to support the work of the traditional medical wisdom. So much of our reading pointed to a positive attitude as a major contributor to healing that we did not neglect the spiritual aspects of her healing.

We truly believed she would be healed. But our faith did not depend on her wellness, though we sought every way possible to restore her health. Jean discovered a new serenity in her faith that allowed her to understand the meaning of "Thy will be done." She frequently explained to her doctor that life with hope is a much better life, no matter how short, than one with despair.

The approach to her illness had to be an approach to the whole person: body, mind, and spirit. The mind and the spirit play such an important role in the growth, development, and healing of the body. We were determined to use every resource at our command, but especially the power of prayer.

Now, two years later, Jean is once again running full speed ahead. She completed the operation which successfully removed five tumors from her liver. She is now free of medication and malignancy according to the past two six-month CAT scans.

The effort to come to grips with the evils of cancer and the experience of confronting social and political evils in society has all been enlightened by our sensitivity to the hand of God moving anonymously and mysteriously through our lives and relationships. None of the success and survival that we have enjoyed over these past decades would have been possible without understanding and sensitivity to the power and presence of God in our daily existence.

Granny's Bag
Atara

When I was a little girl, I'd wonder why my granny and her sister, who were devoted Baptists, would tiptoe back from the Ms. Lady's house carrying a shopping bag full of candles, herbs, incantations, and other tools of divining the present, past, and future. "Granny's got a little something in her bag," she'd whisper to me. It wasn't until I became an astrologer that I realized that the tools and information in Granny's bag could help them heal the sick and maybe even raise the dead. Yet, they had to hide this important part of who they were from everyone, including their own family, or risk being ridiculed and shunned by a society and a community that was not ready to accept the spiritual messages that shopping bag contained.

"Come here, girl," she said to me as I peeked behind the kitchen door. I was the only one in the family who was curious about her bag. I went over to Granny and asked her what was in it. She said, "All the wonders and magic of our African ancestors. They used this stuff to heal the sick and get answers to questions." I sat at her kitchen table, wide-eyed.

"Listen close, baby, cause you need to know what's about to happen in the days to come. We about to move into the next dispensation called the Age of Aquarius. It's gonna be a time when our people reclaim our former greatness. See, we been in denial of who we really are. That's why folks feel like they got to pretend like they're scared of my bag."

"Who are we, Granny?" I asked.

"We the original peoples of this planet. We the mothers and fathers of every race of people. Even the scientists are saying that now."

"Wow!" But as I thought about the poverty in my neighborhood and how bad off some Black people were, I began to wonder why so many of us had sunk so low.

"To understand that, baby girl, you got to understand the history of the world—from an astrological perspective.

"Since the beginning of time, each great cycle from Pisces (moving counterclockwise) to Pisces had a major theme, an idea that was acted out by the original peoples—us, that is.

"The Age of Taurus (4220 B.C. to 2160 B.C.) was about money and keeping up with the Joneses. Africans ruled Egypt during that time, and the Great Pyramid and other monuments were built.

"During the Age of Aries (2160 B.C. to 1 A.D.), leadership and war were the major themes. During this time there were many great African kings who conquered and built great nations. But Aries is the time for new leadership, so the Aryans gained control.

"The age we're in now is Pisces (1 A.D. to 2160 A.D.). We've been in Pisces for the last 2,000 years. According to astrology and different religions, an African named Jesus ushered in this age.

"Now, when you look at the Pisces symbol, you see two fish—one going upstream, the other going downstream. The upstream themes of Pisces are creativity in the arts, meditation, compassion, karma, martyrdom, priests, ministers, psychics. The downstream themes of Pisces are drugs, alcohol, con artists, slavery, ghettoes, dependency, welfare, pimps, and prostitutes."

"Granny, that sounds like what a lot of Black folks are going through!" I said.

"That's right, but remember, we act out the upstream too, not just the downstream. Looky here, child." Granny opened her magical bag and pulled out some herbs and incense. "This here's the same frankincense and myrrh that the three Magi (wasn't nothing but astrologers) used to cleanse the upstream and downstream vibrations surrounding his birth." I didn't understand half of what Granny was saying, but it didn't matter. I loved the soft, velvet country sound of her voice. She made everything sound so exciting and mysterious. "And you know that Star of Bethlehem we sing about in church at Christmas time?"

"Uh huh."

"Wasn't nothing but a planetary alignment, child. Led those three Magi right to the spot where Jesus was born."

"Oh."

"We Black people, we got to look at Jesus' life. His folks had to run away from their home, NO ROOM signs like WHITE ONLY signs. Then, when He got older, He overthrew the system, got whipped and hung on a cross. Now child, who do that sound like to you?"

"Black people?"

"Yep, Black people. On the downstream side, we had it pretty bad with slavery, sharecropping, welfare, and the like. On the upstream, we gotta learn how to love ourselves and each other. Jesus chose surrender over rebellion and love over hate. Yet, he could be militant when it came down to protecting children and old women like me."

"You ain't old, Granny," I said.

"That's what you say! You sweet, though."

"What about the miracles, Granny?" That was my favorite part of the Bible.

"Oh, yeah! He said we could do everything He did and more if only we believed we could. Jesus' life was like a road map showing us the way.

"Now there were some who were jealous of Jesus. They scrambled His message and changed His skin color, which left the world in chaos and confusion. Just like they killed Malcolm X and Martin Luther King because they were dedicated to raising the consciousness of Black folks, they killed Jesus for the same reason.

"Baby, now listen and listen good to what I'm 'bout to tell you: It is no coincidence that Jesus' final message was raising Himself from the dead. We gonna have to do the same if we ever gonna get out of this mess. We first peoples. The world cannot move forward without us giving them the blueprint. *We got the answer*, and it is deep in our souls. They calls us the Sleeping Giant 'cause we don't even know we got the answer.

"When we remember how to use our dreams, music, meditation, trance states, herbs, and other things to heal and move closer to God, then the whole world will change for the better. I see it happening now, slowly but surely. Folks may talk out loud against my bag, but in secret, they want to know what's in it to heal themselves or know the future. In your day and age, baby, people will be more open. They won't be so scared of Granny's bag. Shoot, most folks'll have their own bags."

"Granny, what's it gonna be like when I grow up?"

"Aw, girl, it's gonna be something, maybe a little scary. White folks gonna be studying melanin like crazy, cause they gonna need the protection from the sun real bad. Since we the first peoples with a motherload of the stuff, they gonna be studying us more than ever before.

"Africans are gonna combine technology stuff with natural intuition and creativity, and the world has never seen such genius. We gonna come back in a big way.

"Mostly, I see the Sleeping Giant waking up. We got access to information in the cosmic places, so we'll be able to heal ourselves and the rest of humanity."

Granny got up and walked over to the refrigerator to pour us some juice. Her back to me, I sneaked a peak in her old bag, and what I saw stunned me. I thought I saw *stars*.

Angels of Light and Love
Y. A. Folayan

He told me to go home and live my life. I was dumbfounded. Although I sat in that sterile box of a room watching that very young, very white man out of the coolness and calmness of the eye of a storm that had yet to break, inside I was furious. And dumbfounded. "You can have children with no problem," he replied when my beau, Malki, asked about the possibility of my becoming pregnant. "You can live a normal life. If you have any questions, call me." A normal life? How could I live a normal life when I could no longer walk the mile and a half from my apartment to the university?

I walked out of the doctor's office, with its bare, stark, white walls, in awe of that young man's words. "Go home and live your life the way you always have." Yeah, right. Not only could I not walk the three to four miles a day that was a part of my daily routine, but I could not walk with groceries or any heavy bags. I could not properly see. I had a pinched nerve in the back of my left eye, and let Malki tell it, I couldn't walk a straight line. And stairs whipped my butt good.

On Thursday, October 29, 1992, I was diagnosed with multiple sclerosis, a disease that attacks the central nervous system. A disease that creates a short in the body's electrical system. A disease that has no cure.

I was twenty-three years old, one hundred sixty miles away from home, from family, and my boyfriend of eight months. And I was in the second year of a master's degree program at the University of Wisconsin, Madison.

At some point during a depression that lasted a year, I did a lot of praying. I made general pleas to the universe, to the ancestors, to my spirit guides, to God, for help. I asked to be saved from sinking into an abyss of madness, sadness, and feelings of doom. It didn't occur to me to ask for the help I would need to sustain myself. It didn't even occur to me to pack my bags and go home to my parents where I would not have had to worry about getting groceries, doing laundry, or cooking. I wasn't even in the mind frame to think about how I would finish my thesis. It was like I'd received the "Do not pass go" card in a game of Monopoly. However, as general as my prayers were, the universe heard my cry, and responded with more than I asked for.

My friend Isobel is from Dominique, by way of England. She was a first-year graduate student in the Afro-American Studies department, and she was turning out to be truly a godsend. One night while she visited me, she suggested that we go to her friend Lakshmi's house. I can be very antisocial at times and did not want to go. However, Spirit had a plan and Isobel convinced me to go. I sat in Lakshmi's kitchen and talked with her mother who had been living with MS for ten years. Her mother was white, and I felt uncomfortable talking to her about my condition. Socializing with white people outside of class was not my MO, but there were greater forces at work. Liz asked me if my friends were helping me. "You know your friends should be helping you. If you can't do the laundry, then they should do it for you. Once a week, or whatever you agree on, they should help." I thought, wow, she's a bit much. I was taken aback because Isobel was sitting there, and I don't like asking people for help. Girlfriend patted and rubbed my hand and, with great sincerity, asked me if I needed her help. With difficulty and graciousness, I said yes. She had been coming to sit with me pretty regularly anyway, so we worked out a schedule, and she did my laundry. I sorted, she washed, and we folded.

Before Isobel and I worked out a weekly schedule, my boyfriend did the laundry and went grocery shopping on his biweekly visits. It was a plan that worked out pretty well. I was grateful that he was in my life, willing to help with whatever I needed. (And of course I was watching him, taking notes for future reference and keeping score.)

My fellow classmate and newfound friend Sharon, a Jamaican-American woman who was also in the Afro-American Studies department, called me one night. "Yo, Y.A., how you eatin', girlfriend? How you gettin' groceries?" I laughed as the New York in her burst through her usually academic demeanor. I told her about Malki's biweekly visits, and she told me that she would call me when she went to the store to see if I needed anything in between his treks to Madison. We too worked out a schedule. On Fridays, she would call, I would give her a list of things to buy, and she would bring them over. And yes, I reimbursed her. Sometimes I would open the front door and a bag of groceries, my mail from the Afro-American Studies department, a note, books from the library, something, would be waiting for me. And when our friend Abena bought a used car, she let Sharon use it to drive me to the doctor (which was a ten-dollar cab ride, one way), to the store, or to the movie theater.

I was fortunate. Blessings continued to rain on me. I was at a birthday party for Sharon, when a Jamaican sister I didn't know very well told me she would call me to see if she could be of some assistance. Now, I am a little Black girl from the south side of Chicago. I grew up looking suspiciously at kindness. Especially from virtual strangers. My experiences had taught me not to expect kindness or sustained assistance from my "sisters," so I did not take Gloria seriously until she called the following Friday asking how she could be of help. I thought to myself, "Damn, she's serious," and I thanked the universe for watching over me. Since I was still doing research for my thesis and Gloria lived across the street from the library, she would bring me books. Once, she walked that mile and a half from campus to my house with two milk crates full of books. I don't remember how she did it, but God bless her little self.

My sister-friends did not just run errands for me. They kept me company. One friend just came to talk poetry and bring me king-sized Snickers bars. We were each other's support group in an environment that was not always nurturing. It was academic, white, and at times, it was fierce. I had suspected a community of women was powerful, but I had never *known* it. My experiences with the sisters opened up a world to me that, while foreign, was also familiar. I knew that African-descent women came from a tradition that states we must look out for our own. I *know* now that "I am because we are."

I finished my master's thesis and, more important, I didn't go hungry or crazy because I was sent daughters of light and love to help ease my load. My last day in Madison was emotion-filled. As Malki and I packed my apartment up, Sharon came over to say good-bye. There were no tears, but my heart was breaking. When she left, I laid my head on Malki's chest and cried. Later, Isobel and Gloria came by, and Sharon came back. They didn't leave until the truck pulled out of the driveway. Words cannot express the gratitude I have for those sisters. I can't even explain how much I miss then. They opened my eyes to many things, spiritually, emotionally, and intellectually.

I thank the Divine Mother for initiating me into this order of sisterhood.

Two Women and a Little Olive Oil
Rita Coburn Whack

Arms that hugged too tight, fingers that made biscuits rise, and knees that knelt in prayers calling out my name were some of the woman things I was raised with. Older, most often spiritual, and ample enough to press new life into a crying girl with a cut knee or a hampered spirit, the women of my childhood kissed their spirits into me. I did like most children, became greedy and began to look for more of a good thing.

During my search, inside our family and out into the neighborhood around me, I found reality. Women came in all types. There were those that grew like oak trees, stable enough to offer increasing shades of comfort as time went by. But I also noticed weaker ones. They showed me who not to be like, that weakness was possible but not preferable, and with lots of love weak limbs could be turned into strong branches.

Prior to my teens, I settled into big bosoms, soft laps, and tender arms without question. As I got older and saw women in emotional pain, as close as my sister and as distant as Erica Kane in *All My Children*, I decided to simply respect them all, love the ones I could, give the others a pass, but always, keep my ears cleared and my heart open. All women were teachers. Whenever my feelings were shattered under the fire of a friendship turning sour, my mother would say, "She was only a so-called friend." In time I learned to agree and kept on.

By the time I hit my thirties, I was married, had two children, and was riding high in woman love when I heard about Berniece. I was attending a church in south suburban Chicago and a girlfriend described a deacon whom she thought I'd like. I listened, but from what I could tell, Berniece was a little too charismatic for me. She fit the description of women I loved the most, but she had also crossed the line.

Now, the Bible, Jesus, and Church were never questions in my mind. I had been raised to believe in them all. The women I'd loved had prophesied the future, gathered in prayer and teaching, helped build Bible camps for children, told you who was dead before the phone rang, and watched spirits travel between the worlds as long as I could remember. But I'd heard Berniece did something they didn't do. She anointed people with oil. Accuse me of splitting hairs, but there were some things I just didn't go for. I decided to keep my distance, only to find myself working with Berniece at the church's Vacation Bible School that summer.

I was teaching a raucous bunch of nine- and ten-year-olds, among whom my daughter, Christine, and son, Lee, caused their share of the commotion. Berniece taught an adult class but held the morning devotion for everyone. On the first day she had the nerve to lay hands on people. Ugh! Inwardly I recoiled. Outwardly I couldn't even manage a smile. She called me on it by quoting chapter and verse. ". . . God didn't give us a spirit of fear, but of love, power and a sound mind." I knew about that and I didn't need no Berniece to tell me.

As summer ended I began to attend 6 A.M. prayer service once or twice a week. Often I stood near or next to Berniece. When she held my hand or I heard her voice, I felt a familiar power. I was both attracted to her and made uncomfortable by my dislike of her. After a month or two I knew I was going to have to confront my feelings or stop coming to the service. Kind of hard to pray with somebody you don't like.

One Sunday, I approached Berniece. Somewhere I felt my aunt, Mama Mae Mae say, "If you gon' tell it, tell it true." Doubt countered, how do you say you don't like somebody to their face, if you do that they'll turn their back on you. Then, I remembered my mother saying, "You can't miss what you don't measure."

"Berniece," I said, touching her arm and losing my nerve. Then I remembered the way Miss Josephine always urged me to go on. "Now hear me what I'm saying to you."

"Berniece," I repeated. "I have to tell you something. I don't like you." That slipped, she didn't move, just smiled and waited. "But, I'm attracted to the way you pray and I'd like you to come to my house for lunch. I want to prepare a meal for you." She didn't look shocked; we talked a little more, made arrangements, and exchanged numbers.

From my garden I pulled ripe red tomatoes, tender new leaves of red, bibb, and black seeded Simpson lettuce, pinched the top basil leaves, cut oregano, and snipped parsley. I made bread in the bread machine, pasta with the Cuisinart, used the good olive oil for the pesto, set the table with china, and used crystal wine goblets for pink ginger ale.

When Berniece sat at my table, I found part of an aunt whom I'd loved and now, since her passing, could only cherish in the heirlooms of her thoughts and prayers. I saw the honesty of my mother dressed in a similar humor. When Berniece left I saw myself in her walk. It was more a sashay, confident sash and sway released in full, fabulous hips. I knew it would take me years, but I planned to walk like that. After what Berniece called "my meal" we talked often and prayed up whole lists of things. I'd write down what I wanted, we'd pray, later she'd say, "Guess you can tear that list up."

Winter came, Chicago style, cold till bitter, the crunch of frozen snow crisp underfoot. Thermometers dropped until going outside was left for must-dos. I was working on a television special for African American history month when I got a call from the school. My son wasn't feeling well, pains raced up and down his left side. Two doctor visits found

Lee and I in a neurologist's office seated across from a foreign doctor who either didn't know American customs or lacked simple manners.

"See the X ray," he said. "See the white spots on your son's brain." My son held his head in his hands.

"Oh no," he said in a voice filled with melancholy. "What's wrong with me?"

"Excuse me, Doctor," I said with chill and ice of my own. A woman or a man worth his salt would not have begun such diagnosis with my son in the room. I assured my son everything would be fine and told him to wait outside with his sister. The so-called professional in the room didn't miss a beat.

"The radiologist's findings and the white scar tissues on this X ray show that your son has multiple sclerosis."

I heard his words through muffled ears, his mouth continued to move as if he were asking me if I wanted sugar for my tea, then it stopped, waiting for a response.

The rest of that day was comprised of the female movements we learn by rote. Smile and deflect terrible truths from children, prepare meals, set up the VCR, assign chores. Do what you have to until you can get away and lock the bedroom door, turn the water on in the bathtub to absorb the noise, and cry. I'm not a quick-to-sob sister by nature; my husband offers up far more boo-hoos than I, but on this day I cried unaccepting tears. Who did that man think he was talking to? What did some white spots think they were going to do to my son's brain? Nothing. I decided against panic and prepared to tell my husband when he got home. This was not phone call information. Nothing, I kept repeating. But, I was afraid.

Days went by. At night I went into Lee's room and slept with my hands on his head, prayers moving through my lips. I called Berniece. She listened like I imagine women have listened to each other for centuries, with the delicate lace of patience and compassion in their silence. Story finished, she said, "You know what you're gon' to have to do?"

"No," I said and asked, "what?"

"Anoint him with oil."

Ugh!

"Anoint him with oil?" Just the thought was making me a little heated myself.

"Yes. I know you got some, 'cause you used it when you made my meal."

I thought about it, but my days were filled with making doctors' appointments between research, writing a script, and calling for test results. A case of MS for a child so young is not common, and Dr. No Manners started to display an eerie excitement after a confirming MRI. My husband and I were seeking a second opinion as the day of the final test, a spinal, neared. One parent would be allowed in the room during the procedure and able to spend the night. We decided it would be my husband. We'd called our church and Reverend Bundy was sent out to pray at 4:30 before the 5 P.M. appointment at a hospital five minutes away. I got the olive oil down from the cabinet and poured some in the cap of the bottle with a tremble, wondering how I was going to explain this to my husband and our son, not to mention Reverend Bundy. Fortunately for us all, Reverend Bundy said, "I have some oil here and I'd like to anoint your son."

I was relieved. My husband was open and we asked Lee how he felt about all this. He said he was comfortable with it.

Later at the hospital, I prayed and paced while my two boys were in the room with the doctor. In less than a half hour, he came out smiling. "It is very clear liquid," he told me. "This is a good sign."

Four days later, the doctor was amazed. "Not one white blood cell in fluid, it is not MS. Maybe it was some type of virus or something." My husband and I held each other. When we got home we prayed, smothered our son with kisses, Dad took him out, I made all his favorite foods, and Christine was extra nice to her brother for two days.

That Sunday, Berniece and I hugged. She smiled and threw her hands up in the air, talking to God, walking away, sashaying with the hips of my future. Now, when I cook rice, boil water for pasta, make salad dressing, or any such thing that calls for a little olive oil, I remember. And sometimes I throw my hips slowly from side to side, and watch the oil swirl into another part of my meal.

God and Your Dreams
Wintley Phipps

One night not long ago, I had a stark, vivid dream. In my dream, I was a little boy again, no more than four or five years old, and I was frolicking alone in a garden of aromatic flowers, skipping through blossoms aflame with color. I knew again the solace I had found only in my childhood dreams, and I didn't want to let it go.

Suddenly, I felt a gentle tap on my shoulder. It was unlike any touch I had ever felt, full of love and authority. I knew instinctively it was the Lord.

"You find sweet pleasure in your dreams of yesterday," he said. "Come with me. Let me show you my garden. Let me show you the future I have prepared for you."

He put his arms around me and led me to a garden where, as far as my eye could see, pure white, thornless roses grew. Each petal, perfectly sculptured, spoke of the love and care with which he nurtured every rose. What a sight it was. His garden!

"Look at my flowers," he said, as he motioned over that garden of pristine beauty. "Each rose holds a dream I carry in my heart for each of my children. One of these roses is for you."

Then he reached down, plucked the most beautiful rose I had ever seen, and gave it to me. As I held it, I felt so blessed, so fortunate, not just because of the gift, but because I knew it came from the hand of the King, the royal monarch of the universe.

"Son," he said, as I firmly clasped his gift, "hold this rose close to your heart. It will give your life the sense of purpose I wish for it to have. Wintley, I have a dream for your life, but it's up to you to believe that I can make it come true."

Then his voice became deeply earnest and filled with caution. "Listen carefully, my son. Unfaithfulness and sinful habits can cause you to forfeit the future I have prepared for you. Don't let sin defile the beauty of your future. This thornless white rose is a sign of the promise I make with you. Soon I am coming again for you and this rose. And I want you to be ready to return with me to your heavenly home."

As he spoke, I could almost feel that moment when we would stand together before the mansion he has prepared for me. What a precious moment it will be when I kneel on heaven's soil and plant my rose in that sacred place. There I will plant my dreams firmly in the fertile soil of heaven, where I will hear no echoes of doubt and confusion and where I will become exactly what he wants me to be.

"Oh," I whispered, "if only I could keep this dream alive."

He whispered back, "You can, with my help."

Did you know that God is a dreamer?

The original visionary.

When he dreams, constellations are born.

When he dreams, stars twinkle in the sky.

When he dreams, flowers ooze out of the ground and when they behold His glory they blush—in technicolor.

But did you know that when God the father dreams, he also dreams about you, his child? Did you know that he has a plan, a dream for your life?

The power in God's dream for you is limitless. To see that dream and act upon it can change your immediate physical circumstance, even mold and alter your destiny. Nothing can stand in the way of a dream birthed in the mind of God.

Take from his hand your dream, your white rose. And trust his plans for you. "For I know the plans I have for you," declares the Lord, "plans to prosper you and not to harm you, plans to give you hope and a future" (Jer. 29:11).

God has a dream for you. It's up to you to fit into his plan. God will even use miracles to make your dreams come true. God's plans for your life are far beyond the limitations of your mind.

Only when you surrender your dreams to God can you find the true fulfillment of those dreams. When you put your life into God's hands and let him take charge, your dreams become absorbed by the dream that God has for you. God makes himself responsible for your success and for making your dreams come true. When you give yourself and all that you are into God's hands, then you can expect to see wonderful things happen.

A Prayer for Children
Marian Wright Edelman

O God, we pray for children who woke up this morning in dens of dope rather than in homes of hope, with hunger in their bellies and hunger in their spirits, without parents or friends to care for, affirm, and lovingly discipline them.

Help us to welcome them in our hearts and communities.

We pray for children who have no one to pray for them or protect and guide them and who are being abused or neglected right now by parents who themselves often were abused or neglected.

Help us to welcome them in our hearts and communities.

We pray for children who are sick from diseases we could have prevented, who are dying from guns we could have controlled, and who are killing from rage we could have averted by loving attention and positive alternatives.

Help us to welcome them in our hearts and communities.

We pray for children struggling to live to adulthood in the war zones of our cities, who plan their own funerals and fear each day will be their last. We mourn for the thousands of children whose life journeys have already ended too violently and too soon.

Help us to welcome them in our hearts and communities.

We pray for children who are born with one, two, three, or more strikes already against them—too tiny to live, too sick with AIDS, too addicted to alcohol or cocaine or heroin to thrive.

Help us to welcome them in our hearts and communities.

We pray for girl children having children without husbands or steady friends or lifelines of support, who don't know how to parent and who need parenting themselves. And we pray that teen and adult fathers will take more responsibility for the children they father.

Help us to welcome them in our hearts and communities.

We pray for children who are born into and grow up in poverty without a seat at America's table of plenty; for youths whose only hope for employment is drug dealing, whose only sense of belonging is gangs, whose only haven is the streets, and whose only tomorrow is prison or death.

Help us to welcome them in our hearts and communities.

We pray for children and youths in every community struggling to make sense of life, confused by adults who tell them one thing and do another;

who tell them not to fight but who fight and tell them not to take drugs while taking drugs.

Help us to welcome them in our hearts and communities.

O God, we pray for children from whom we expect too little and for those from whom we expect too much; for those who have too little to live on and for those with so much they appreciate little; for children afflicted by want and for children afflicted by affluence in a society that defines them by what they have rather than by who they are—Your loving precious gift.

Help us to welcome them in our hearts and communities.

We pray for ourselves as parents, teachers, preachers, and leaders, that we will help solve rather than cause the problems our children face, by struggling to be worthy of emulation, since we teach each minute by example.

O God, we pledge to pray and work to save our children's lives.

Help us.

O God, we pledge to pray and work to protect our children's dreams.

Help us.

O God, we pledge to pray and work to rekindle our children's hopes.

Help us.

O God, we pledge to pray and work to rebuild our children's families.

Help us.

O God, we pledge to pray and work to create a sense of community and security for our children.

Help us.

O God, we pledge to pray and work to instill in our children a knowledge and appreciation of their traditions and heritage.

Help us.

O God, we pledge to pray and work to leave no child behind.

Help us.

A Miracle of Love
JoAnn Long

It was the 1980s and the AIDS virus discovery and exposure was yet new in our community and I was walking through my valley of the shadow of death and fearing the evil. Truthfully speaking, I felt more like I was crawling through it. Nevertheless, I was moving, determined to get through.

My husband, Tracy, was in the hospital fighting for his life and the doctor's report of his condition was resounding over and over again in my mind. It was not good: HIV positive and its possible/likely fatal outcome—the statistics! The specialists in his field could not offer us any hope and expressed grave concern for me.

Hurting and angry, I questioned how I could be confronted with such a monumental situation which was bigger than life, an intrusion, an invasion of my private world, my home, marriage, and family. I thought, surely not my husband—not me! Why me?

I was filled with shock and grief. I waited for something more to be said—some explanation, perhaps. Something! It did not come. I was not really prepared for this, I thought. Then, as if someone had pushed a video replay button, I began to hear words of advice that had been spoken to my parents approximately twenty years ago as I was coming of age. It was a different time, a different setting, but those words began to replay in my mind even louder than the hopelessness of the doctor's words and the fear of the situation—what I was feeling.

This is the wise counsel of that individual. She said that as my parents let go, I would develop and mature as a beautiful woman. She perceived that even as a child, I flourished under pressure best when I was not petted, pampered, or smothered with needless pity or sympathy. Through difficulties, I would draw from my own resources and make it.

As I remembered these words, I not only drew strength from within, but I discovered I had the courage to embrace my destiny. What I encountered, experienced, and lived through leaves me awestruck even to this day.

November 1986, Tracy LaMar Allen died. After his death, I experienced loneliness such as one could never even imagine. Our courtship and marriage was a sum total of twenty-five years filled with joys and trials; struggles and successes; good days and bad (so many of the bad days toward the end). He had chosen to live part of his life anonymously as a bisexual (functioning as both and with both: male and female). The confirmed news of this, as well as the consequences thereof was devastating to him, our families, and me. He was HIV positive and dying with an AIDS-related disease. The pronouncement of death came and I was shattered. I remember that day vividly. My hopes, my dreams, my desires of living "happily ever after" had died, perished before my very eyes, and what awful perishing it was. I was torn within. Mentally and emotionally I was confused. I had married young, innocent, and trusting. I had given myself so unequivocally without reservation or inhibitions to a marriage that I expected to last a lifetime. Looking back, I was never inclined to cautious restraint in our relationship as others would express their knowledge or opinions. I loved him, believed in him, and believed that our love could withstand any test or trial. Unbelievably, after all these years, it was over. Our marriage had ended.

He was dead! I thought this nightmare was over, I wanted to hope again—a fresh start, build a new life, but I plunged head on into post-traumatic stress. I had countless agonizing concerns for my physical well-being, and my mental and emotional being was under siege. To top all of that, along with the grief I was experiencing, I was isolated socially as a result of the humiliating and embarrassing occurrences tied to his sickness and death. I was so lonely.

My husband was a minister—double jeopardy! After discovering the truth, learning of his life of anonymity during his illness, I acquiesced to his request not to share what was happening with family and others for the sake of the children and the church, and to avoid further embarrassment and ridicule. I loved him. I respected his individuality and privacy. He made a futile attempt to protect me and our children by choosing to die incognito, but the news got out and I was accused of not turning state's evidence and supporting him in a lifestyle that constituted double standards. I lost much physically, socially, materially. And, oh, the pain!

During that time of aloneness and loneliness, once again the video replay button was pushed and I remembered during meditation that prior to all of this happening, I had been given the assurances of marriage—a good marriage. A whole marriage was part of my great destiny. I would have a New Life, a New Husband, a New Beginning. And even though there were people and things missing from my life, I was not to complain, for I had substance. Substance within. Momentarily, I had stopped teaching, talking, sharing, etc. I thought about the movie *The Color Purple* (Tracy and I had gone to see it during his illness on opening night at the theater) and the scene when Sophia (Oprah Winfrey) says at the dining room table, "Sophia's back! Sophia's back! Pass the potatoes."

I was back and I was ready to make a comeback. The only way I knew to make a comeback was to go on. Slowly but surely, I began to accept speaking engagements, seminars, workshops, etc.

Then it happened! One Saturday afternoon in 1989 while speaking to the Midwest Clergy Association, I met the man I was to marry—my future husband, though I did not know it at the time. He had observed and admired me, asking for an introduction. From our first meeting, which was so coincidental to me, and during the occasional times of our being together, I found myself filled with a whole succession of emotions—amazement (more at myself than him), excitement, fear, joy, love. I knew nothing about him, knew nothing about his background and coupled with the fact that I was afraid to allow myself to become vulnerable to another man again, I acted with great caution. After what I had come through, it was hard to trust.

I feared close personal involvement and quickly resolved to avoid this stranger, for I did not have to respond to him. It was too risky. He did not have my home address or telephone number and I was not giving it to him. That did not deter him in his pursuit, and he gained knowledge as to my church home and began to pursue—and how he pursued—such a gentleman (a gentle man), expressing loving care not only for me, but my children. I vowed to keep this relationship superficial (in spite of his gestures that were so compelling) and maintain my own agenda. As time progressed and barriers began to come down, I found myself at ease with his wholesome character and personality. I remember telling my dad and others how refreshing, soothing, and comforting he was to me.

I was on the road to recovery, healing, and restoration, and I felt this was the beginning of a safe, healthy, and uninjurious relationship. I was not intending to think seriously, feel seriously, or be serious. Another intimate relationship? No! I don't think so! How did we get on the subject of marriage?

Yes, I had hoped to build a new life, with the promise of a new husband, my believing God for him—but was it him? He was asking me to marry him and amazingly, I was saying, "Yes."

Then it happened! Feelings of the past surfaced. What I was feeling emotionally was almost overwhelming. I was torn between excitement and fear. One of my most compelling, deep-seated concerns was the possibility of deception again. What if I was being deceived? Should I risk loving again, letting myself go emotionally? I had been betrayed, dishonored, and ultimately abandoned before; I was not willing to put myself in a position of vulnerability to another man's emotions or actions that would wound me and cause me to suffer again.

Foolishly, I began to pull back, retreat, and test our wholesome relationship in ways that I should not—which almost ended in disaster.

I had to become willing to let go of my past, forgive, and trust once again. I had a choice: believe God's promise of satisfaction and fulfillment or spend the remainder of my life in fear and loneliness. I was plain old scared. I began to realize that no process of reasoning would work. I could not figure it out or reason out in my detailed mind, and my heart was overwhelmed; I began to cry unto One that is higher than me for wisdom, understanding, and guidance. Once again, I was encouraged to embrace my destiny, to trust and allow God to work things out. I knew this man whom I had known for only a year was my husband and I was to be his good thing, his wife, his helpmate. I was settled in an area in my heart and mind where doubt and fear had no access and could not intrude. Marrying John was to be a wonderful part of his great destiny and mine.

We were married June 1990, and one of the most endearing gifts that John gave to me at our wedding ceremony was tears. His impassioned, genuine tears flowed unabashedly from his eyes and down his face as I walked down the aisle and into his arms at the altar as his bride. Later, in our honeymoon suite, he told me that his heart was overwhelmed with love and joy to find such a *virtuous woman*, that I was so beautiful as his bride, and how much he loved me.

Often I hear, "How did you meet him?" "You are married to such a good man." "Where did he come from?"

In the Gospel according to St. John, chapter one, verse six, you will read these words: "There was a man sent from God, whose name was John."

Something Wonderful to Behold
Dawn Turner Trice

My daughter, Hannah, was born on Christmas Day, 1994, incredibly healthy and the mirror image of my husband, David. Though it was uncanny how her face held so many of his features, it was her eyes that distinguished her most. David and I both stood in awe of Hannah's eyes: dark brown, marble-like and so immense they seemed capable of swallowing up the entire universe. Part of this, we certainly understood, was simply that Hannah was our only child, and first-time parents often marvel at the slightest of things.

Fourteen months after Hannah's birth, our daughter unexpectedly took gravely ill. She was diagnosed with streptococcal meningitis, a brain infection that could result in death or severe mental retardation if not treated in time.

March 1, 1996, began with a fever. Hannah's pediatrician initially diagnosed her fever as resulting from an ear infection. So the doctor, in routine fashion, prescribed antibiotics. But two nights later, Hannah was not responding to the medicine. She was becoming increasingly lethargic, her neck was stiffening and her eyelids had begun to sag. We rushed her to the emergency room, where she was admitted on the spot and, following a CAT scan, whisked upstairs to the pediatric intensive care unit.

273

Before seeing her, the hospital's chief pediatric neurosurgeon and his assistant led David and me to a fairly nondescript room, the size of a walk-in closet, where the unit's nurses usually took their breaks. We sat down at a small Formica table. The words I'll never forget. The doctor said Hannah's ear infection had made a rare turn into a brain infection. He said her brain had begun to swell. While doctors were doing everything they could to slow the swelling—including putting her in an induced coma—there was nothing man or medicine could do to stop it. The skull, he said, is rigid. When the brain swells, there's no place for it to expand within the skull's cavity. So the victim dies.

David and I left the little room numb, walking like zombies past several beds of children to get to Hannah. She was in an enclosed room in the back of the unit. The bed was high to accommodate a tightrope balance of tubes and wires stretching from monitors to our daughter's splayed arms and legs. She was wearing nothing but a diaper and even her barrettes had been removed and placed atop a cold metal counter. The only thing I could think to tell her was that she came from some strong people. Not necessarily her mother, I thought at the time, but her grandparents. Her great-grandparents. And if she was coming back to us, it would be up to her and God. The doctors, although key, had already admitted their limitations. I took her hand in mine and told her to come this way. I told God that He'd have to help me accept His will. But I assured Him that I needed her more than He did. So I told Hannah once again to run this way.

My husband and I left the room and went out into the waiting room, and, as if by sheer reflex, we began to pray. In the midst of a blasting television and elevator doors that constantly swung open and shut, we begged God to heal Hannah and to return her to us whole. Then we walked to the back of the waiting room where a group of pay telephones lined the wall. I grabbed one and David grabbed another. We began calling friends and family members, everyone whose number we knew by heart, asking them to pray for Hannah.

Soon people all over the country—from Catholics to Jews to Muslims to Jehovah's Witnesses—were praying for our daughter's full recovery. One friend even said she hadn't been on her knees in years but she did so for Hannah.

For four days Hannah lay comatose, her brain teasing at times, slowly decreasing then increasing. For four days we sang to her, massaged her hands and legs, prayed at her bedside. On the fifth day, Hannah definitely was responding to the antibiotics and doctors began slowly waking her up. It was exactly eight days after she was admitted to the hospital that she opened her eyes. With David and me standing over her, we watched as those tiny eyelids fluttered, struggling to part. It was reminiscent of her trying to stand and walk for the first time. Finally Hannah did it, squinting into the light, staring blindly at first beyond our faces. For us, we were experiencing her rebirth. Although at this point doctors still could not determine the overall effect the meningitis would have on Hannah, one visible sign was that her left eye deviated outward and that eyelid also dropped more than the right. But the important thing, the most glorious fact of all, was that Hannah was alive and about to begin her journey back to us.

In all, Hannah's hospital stay was thirty-five days. Each day her progress was exponential. Doctors and nurses were stunned at how well she was doing. Once again she was singing cartoon songs, attempting to feed herself, and playing with her stuffed animals that we'd brought in to give her some semblance of home.

When doctors were certain Hannah was out of danger, they felt freer to tell us the havoc they had seen meningitis wreak. At the same time Hannah was hospitalized, a child in St. Louis, who had been stricken with the same strain of the infection, was doing poorly. The little girl was still slipping in and out of noninduced comas and an eye had been removed. We heard stories of myriad other children who either had not survived or were left severely retarded. Some even had to have limbs amputated.

I look at our daughter now, and it is not clear to me why Hannah's outcome was so very different from that of the other children. We prayed, as I'm certain other parents had prayed. We, too, asked God to guide the doctor's hands. I know our prayers were no more special or specific than anyone else's. So I am in awe as each day she gets stronger and stronger, climbing, running, thriving. And her brain is perfectly intact. The only residue of her illness is that her left eye remains slightly deviated. But it, too, is getting stronger. The truth is, I may never know why Hannah was spared.

This I do know—that God, who gave us our Christmas baby, once again has given us a tremendous gift. The gift of perspective. An opportunity to realize that "the good life" does not occur at a time, often a tomorrow, when all our bills are paid, our bodies are perfectly proportioned, and all our worries run like water into the shade. Each day when I look into Hannah's eyes I know that I am living the good life. And I understand that I am staring into something far greater than I ever could have imagined before. I'm viewing her indomitable spirit; her feistiness; her will to survive. In her eyes, I see hope and endless possibilities. And most of all, I am witnessing one of God's miracles. His power is on some days incomprehensible, but on every day something wonderful to behold.

A Warning Dream
(Spring 1984)

Jocelyn Rials

It is my wedding day, and I am dressed in a beautiful gown. I approach the door of the church sanctuary, when suddenly I have to pee. So off I run to the wing of the church that has a women's rest room. When I open the door I immediately see a covered whirlpool/Jacuzzi a few feet in on the floor. This is shocking at first, but I keep going because I have to "go."

As I near the stalls, I notice an open window with a view of an Olympic-sized pool. At the far end of the pool is one lone brother, just standing there neck high in cold water. I know this man. In fact, I am seriously in love with him (or so I think). Then it dawns on me that if he is in the pool and I'm in love with him, who am I about to marry?

Something's not right, so I jump up and run to the door, when, to my surprise, the same covered whirlpool/Jacuzzi in the floor is now uncovered and is whirling warm water. I wonder what this means. How and when did this all happen?

I run out the door, stuffing my white wedding dress down inside of my blue jeans, and run out of the church. Needless to say, I don't get married.

This dream was a warning to me, giving me an opportunity to see on a superconscious level that even though I wanted to get married, neither I nor my boyfriend was ready. Oh, if only I had paid attention! We all receive inner guidance through dreams, if only we would listen. Our dreams can truly be helpful and can help us avoid much pain and heartache.

Fear often brings on the need to urinate, and in my dream I had to "go" badly. Deep down, although I wanted to get married, I was deeply afraid, and my dream reflected that.

My dream used the water in the whirlpool/Jacuzzi and pool to symbolize emotions and sexuality. The whirlpool was covered, which meant that I was emotionally unavailable. My mate, bless his heart, was standing in an Olympic-sized pool up to his neck in *cold water*. My dream was trying to tell me as plainly as possible that this man was emotionally cold. In the entire pool of emotional/sexual possibilities, he was unable to move. He was in an emotional rut.

Interestingly, when the whirlpool/Jacuzzi re-presented itself as warm and flowing, instead of stepping in to relax and refresh myself, I chose instead to stuff my white wedding gown into my blue jeans and run away. My dream used the blue jeans to show me that I had not yet resolved my issues with my male self—that part of me that goes out into the world and makes an impact, the aggressive, risk-taking part of me. I was not open to receiving warmth and love from a man, a problem that had its roots in my relationship with my father.

Even though my dream showed me my future if I were to marry this man, my ego and our karma would not allow me to release him. So, five years after I had the dream, we married. Divorce was inevitable, however, and we parted in October 1994.

Even though my relationship with this man was troubled because of both of our issues, I learned much about myself while I was with him. What gives me joy is in knowing that the Father has not left us without a Comforter and Guide. If we would just get quiet, listen to, *and heed* what Spirit is saying to us, we would grow and experience joy in our lives. I now trust the Inner Voice with the details of my life, big or small. I trust It with my life.

Opening the Spirit
Karen M. Hurley

My spirit started to open up in late August 1995, on a canoe and camping trip in the Boundary Waters Canoe Wilderness Area (BWCA) located in northern Minnesota. My husband, Richard, and I began our trip driving on Interstate 94 from Chicago, where we live, to Minneapolis, Minnesota. We stayed overnight at my husband's parents' home in suburban Wayzata. The next morning the four of us went shopping for last-minute camping equipment, then Richard and I continued north to Ely. I was excited about this trip, which differed in one significant way from our usual camping and hiking vacations. Instead of touring the wilderness by car, we would travel everywhere by canoe.

On a Tuesday, around mid-morning, we arrived in Ely, a remote town whose one main thoroughfare was lined end-to-end with canoe outfitters. We found our outfitter in a tidy storefront that looked as if it had once been an old-time saloon, near the town's outskirts. A soft-spoken, slender man with a bush red beard issued everything we would need: our BWCA 7-day camping permit, our canoe, three adult-size paddles, two waterproof maps, and two life jackets. His smiling pregnant wife took care of our charges with me, while Richard watched Red Beard load the massive canoe onto the roof of our car.

Back in the car, we drove for about five minutes when we encountered a dead end: we had arrived at Lake One, our entry point to the Boundary Waters. We hauled our sixty-five-pound canoe off the car, packed it full with our camping gear, then carried it to the beach. After parking the car, we were finally ready to row through the wilderness.

Fatigued from our early-morning drive from Minneapolis, Richard shoved us off into the dark, shallow waves of Lake One. Exhilaration took over as I, in the front spot, paddled my first strokes in a canoe in years. We canoed several rods (a rod is a canoe length, equal to approximately sixteen feet), skimming easily on the lake, enjoying using the unfamiliar muscles of the back, shoulders, arms, and abdomen. Our breathing drifted into the rhythm of stroking the water, which felt like silk when you draped your fingernails across it. We became so intoxicated that before long we lost track of where we were going. Soon, we stopped paddling and the boat drifted aimlessly while Richard studied our map. Comparing our actual physical position in the lake to where we appeared to be according to the map coordinates completely disoriented me.

While Richard hunkered over the maps, I rolled my eyes, drained of all my former appreciation for the incredible beauty surrounding us. For a brief intense moment, I hated every island, every lake, every puff of white cloud in my vision. If Richard didn't figure out where we were and where we were going, we couldn't continue, since I had no clue how to navigate around the maze of islands. Eventually, Richard's memory of traversing the lakes and woods of his hometown of Wayzata intuitively kicked in and helped him understand the landscape of the Boundary Waters wilderness.

He told me to paddle left, then right, past some trees, around a big island, and then he said with relief and excitement, "There it is!" Several yards ahead, I saw a narrow embankment that was the only portage linking Lake One to Lake Three. (A portage is a strip of land that connects the lakes.) After a few hard, deep strokes, we heard a scraping against the bottom of the boat. Land! After disembarking, we first ate a few bites of energy bar, because by then the sun had reached its zenith and we were starved.

The portage measured about ten rods, a short distance, but it took us nearly thirty minutes to cross, because we carried the canoe incorrectly. Instead of one person helping the other hitch the canoe upside down, over the head, balanced on the shoulders the way the outfitter demonstrated, we foolishly loaded it down with all our gear, then each grabbed an end. We had to stop every few steps to catch our breaths, since carrying a canoe this way feels like dragging an elephant by its tail.

Finally back in the water, I was so tired and irritable that I was ready to stop at the first available campsite. Since the map indicated the nearest campsite was only about twenty-five rods away from the portage, we decided to check it out. I paddled desperately, like a stranded sea captain lost in a storm for several days who has suddenly caught sight of land. A few minutes later, we ran aground and for the first time that day, I hopped out to pull the rest of the canoe ashore.

Once Richard was standing on dry land, I grabbed one of our packs from the canoe and hiked a few steps past the rocky beach to a sandbox. From there, three high steps led me to a small clearing with smooth, dry grass framed by two huge oaks. I collapsed with my arms and legs spread straight out and my rear end scrunched in the air. I was a turtle sunning itself on a log, happy to be out of the water for a while. Richard laughed at me from his spot underneath the cottonwood tree near the beach. After a few minutes, he got up to set up our tent, a years-old hand-me-down from his elder brother. I turned on my back, my body spread-eagled except for my arms, which were tucked behind my head above the hard ground.

This time, viewing the world from the safety of land, I held more appreciation as I stared at the expansive blanket of sky, the sun brightly burning above. Suddenly, I had the urge to cartwheel, but I stayed put. Then, my body became heavy, and I experienced an underwater sensation like being buried by a flood of warm, briny-sweet Boundary Water.

I felt immense joy at being alive, since I had not been so sure that we would figure out how to navigate around the wilderness. I squeezed my eyes shut, and I silently thanked the Creator for guiding us to the campsite safely.

My eyes opened on the island jutting out directly across the lake, parallel to our island campsite. I noticed its tall pine stands mirrored our own island pines; it seemed they were all in the same family. Minutes passed into late afternoon as I watched what looked like fingertips, the tips of tree branches, scratch the air, as if the wind had a wild, invisible, unbearable itch. I inhaled and exhaled long, expanding my stomach and chest to catch Mother Nature's breath down deep in my lungs. After a while, I stuck a sprig of grass between my back teeth. The green taste was like the smell of the air at the level of a canoe coasting on the lake. I removed the sprig and tucked it in my journal.

A moment later (or it could have been an hour), I found myself no longer consciously thinking about or visually seeing my surroundings. I could no longer hear the normal sounds of my surroundings, either. Singing birds, blowing wind, lapping waves; all these sounds disappeared, or rather were tuned out. I began to hear beyond this noise, tuning in to the earth I was lying on with my body, my gut, instead of with my head.

My body didn't feel like my body anymore either; it was there, but it was not there. It felt like the amplified ear of a tiny creature, like a spider, because the sounds I could hear were very subtle, not sounds humans normally pick up. At the same time, my body also felt like a living-tissue speaker, because it also transmitted the vibrations that it was picking up. The vibrations that my body heard were born from silence; the complete silence of my head, which is normally brimming with thoughts. My head had been dominated by fearful thoughts from almost the moment we had entered Lake One.

Now, with an empty head, I heard my body humming, and I knew that the same sound was being made by everything in my surroundings, the wind, birds, bugs, trees, rocks, water, and grass. The sound was also sensation, which registered like a drum when it makes a beat, and the beat reverberates around, outside, and inside every person who is listening. The listeners are energized into dance, into energy, and in a sense, by translating the sound into dance, they become the beat at the same time.

The silent vibrations or beat that I heard and felt connected me to everything in the universe. Matter manifests itself in an infinite number of shapes with an infinite number of functions. But regardless of the form it takes, all matter is essentially enlivened by the same energy: spirit energy.

My spirit had been tapped open for the first time in my life. Hearing in another dimension, I felt a deep bond with every living thing in the universe that I have held onto since that time. I woke up from my trance in a profound state of joy and grace. The experience had only lasted a few minutes, but it has changed me forever in ways that cannot be articulated. Being able to hear the beat connecting everything in nature was a gift to my soul. It was like learning a new wordless language that everything, even a rock, can understand and speak.

Now, back at home in the city, I have to work harder to listen for the silent beat of the trees, but from time to time, though it is faint, I can still hear it. Even though I don't always know their names, I do recognize families of trees along my train route to work. And I find now that when I pay attention to other beings of nature, whether it's an ant, tree, spider, or bush, I feel inexplicably soothed and rejuvenated. Listening for the subtle sound of nature's drum is a means to open the divine spirit of the universe that enlivens our minds and bodies, and bonds us to our world and everything in it.

A Pyramid Prophecy
Gail Erskine

I see a pyramid pulsating with energy—heavy, oppressive energy, as if something is short-circuiting and stifling its power. Then I hear voices, children's voices, voices of young boys in particular, six, seven, eight years old, crying from within the pyramid. They are trapped and yelling as children do when they are in danger or in trouble. They cry, "Mommy, Mommy, Mommy, Mommy. . . ."

I woke up startled and wrote down the dream. At the time, I put it to the side. It was disturbing and I really didn't understand it. Months later, it became the subject of an experimental video I made in class the following September. My instructor asked us to interpret a dream. This "Mommy-Pyramid" dream immediately came to mind, but I had no real idea of what it meant. I decided to use this project to help me not only document my dream but understand it. Once I committed to this goal, the universe synchronistically brought the players and methods to me.

I met Evangel Mama Dee, poet, writer, lecturer, and community activist, at the State of Illinois building. I had to go there to get a new state ID because I had lost my old one. As the universe would have it, we were waiting in one of those never-ending lines together and struck up a conversation. Mama Dee told me she had attended the Million Man March and had erected a pyramid out there on the grounds. *A pyramid!* I thought. How many people were building pyramids at the March? Not many, if any. Mama Dee also had fasted and prayed in a pyramid she had erected under the viaduct on Chicago's south side where Robert Sandifer was killed by teenage gangsters. Would this woman provide a clue to my dream?

I asked her if she would like to be a part of the video and she consented. It was like meeting a long-lost sister. She has connected her soul to her ancient roots, that OverSoul which I was just now learning how to plug into. It was exciting to watch her speak and teach.

The other speakers in the video were friends from school. I told them I needed to hear the voices of everyday women like themselves for my video. Their responses after editing the footage melded quite well together and a message came through, loud and clear: *Mothers are the key to the healing and building of our people; they are the key to the transference of wisdom and knowledge to the children, male and female.*

When I had this dream, I possessed no understanding of how profound African culture was in religious, social, and governmental areas thousands of years ago. I voraciously read books like the *Destruction of Black Civilization* by Chancellor Williams, the *Metu Neter* by Ra Un Nefer Amen, and an article in *Mo Better News* on "The Numerological Significance of the Divine Mother," which the Black woman represented on earth according to ancient African tradition.

My knowledge of history, culture, religion, and spiritual values of ancient Africa, especially Egypt, increased by leaps and bounds since I had that dream. The dream was sparked by asking questions, asking the Creator, the Divine Mind that knows everything about the past, present, and future to give me insight and it did by the dream, by the people I happened to meet, by the books which were introduced to me by others, and by personal ramblings in book stores. What is most exciting is that other African American women are tuning in to the discovery of the great past within and rising to the occasion of becoming the great champions of the future. Because of this dream, I have decided to become a public school teacher.

Just today, the newspaper announced that Rosa Parks was coming to Chicago to speak to the children. Like her, we must reach the children. We must not give up on them. Black women are hearing the message from the universe today. Everywhere they are responding to the call, *Mommy, Mommy, Mommy.*

The Nguzo Saba for a New Millennium

Created by Maulana Karenga in 1965, the Nguzo Saba provides a culturally relevant philosophical framework upon which our social, cultural, economic, and personal growth programs and strategies can be designed, developed, and implemented. Most of us have become familiar with the seven principles through Kwanzaa (celebration of the first fruits), the African American holiday that falls on December 26 through January 1. Imagine what oases our communities would become if we all began to meditate upon and practice the following principles! What greatness and joy we could achieve!

Umoja (unity)—to strive for and maintain unity in the family, community, nation, and race.

Kujichagulia (self-determination)—to define ourselves, create for ourselves, and speak for ourselves, instead of being defined, named, created by, and spoken for by others.

Ujima (collective work and responsibility)—to build and maintain our community together and to make our sisters' and brothers' problems *our* problems and to solve them together.

Ujamaa (cooperative economics)—to build and maintain our own stores, shops, and other businesses and to profit from them together.

Nia (purpose)—to make as our collective vocation the building and developing of our community in order to restore our people to their traditional greatness.

Kuumba (creativity)—to do always as much as we can, in the way we can in order to leave our community more beautiful and beneficial than when we inherited it.

Imani (faith)—to believe with all our hearts in our people, our parents, our teachers, our leaders, and the righteousness and victory of our struggle.

The People Can Still Fly

Donna Marie Williams

For most of the students in African History class, the lesson was just another recitation of boring stories, dates, and events. But for Regina, Mr. Harper's words were life. She felt herself transported back to a time when great African kings and queens ruled the Motherland. She saw herself as Sheba, Cleopatra, Esat, Nzinga, and Nefatari. The mundane life in the projects faded to just a bad aftertaste as she stood face to face with the Sphinx, the Great Pyramid of Giza, the libraries, temples—the land.

Regina's classmates hated African history. Had no use for slavery or the jungle days, as they put it. They wanted to make fast money, talk about clothes and boys, or exchange makeup tips. Regina felt like a sister from another planet.

The bell rang, and the children grabbed their books and ran out of the classroom. Regina, however, lingered, savoring the lesson and her fantasies.

"You like history, don't you, Regina?" Mr. Harper's voice intruded into her thoughts. Shyly, she gathered her books and held them to her chest. "It's good to see a young person interested in the stories of our past," smiled Mr. Harper.

Regina started to rush out of the classroom, but a thought stopped her. "Mr. Harper, if our ancestors were kings and queens—"

"And farmers and merchants and builders," he said, "and priests and doctors and—"

"Right, if they were all that, and if we're their children, then why are we in such a bad way?" Mr. Harper's smile faded. "Why can't we even get a job?" Regina's eyes were black, deep, and unfathomable. Who knew what memories they held or what sights they might behold tonight?

Mr. Harper knew she was risking something great by this sharing, but something even greater was pushing her to put aside caution. In a culture that revered the ethic of cool—no emotions save anger and rage—she had the courage to feel a full range of emotions. She was different in many ways from her classmates. Her peers looked down on good students, calling them "white acting." Still, Regina had the nerve to love her studies. Many of the rap songs of her generation pushed hopelessness, death, and destruction. Yet, she still had hope and life. Her words rang with a passionate fervor that made Mr. Harper sit up and take notice. She spoke with another emotion too. Longing?

Regina asked, barely above a whisper, "Mr. Harper, what's the secret to the Flight?" Regina clutched her books tightly to her chest as she waited for an answer.

The Flight. Of course he knew what she meant. Grandma Cora told him the story often. Of Africans with wings, of magic words, of escape from white cruelty by air. In fact, hearing "The People Could Fly" over and over again as a child had inspired him to eventually study and teach history. From his grandmother he learned the true purpose of history—not to program people into believing that they were superior or inferior, but to provide clues to help us understand ourselves. History was about self-discovery. History was only one attempt to answer the questions, Who am I? Who are we? What's our purpose?

Regina dropped her books on her desk. "Didn't you once say that myths and legends are most always based on fact?" Mr. Harper nodded, watching her closely. Regina's black eyes were flashing. "This story is told in different ways, but basically it's the same story. There are black slaves being beaten by a white master. Some of the slaves remember the secret of the Flight, the others don't. We're the children of the ones who didn't know. Some old person says some magic words, and the slaves just rise up into the air and fly away," she said wistfully. "Mr. Harper?"

"Yes, Regina?"

"The Flight must be true. We were not meant to live like this." Her outstretched arms encompassed not only the classroom, but the school, the neighborhood, the entire city. "Crack in the hallways, gang banging everywhere, little boys getting shot, little girls getting raped." Her eyes were shiny with tears, but her enormous strength kept them from splashing down her beautiful brown cheeks. "Mothers," she whispered, ashamed but compelled to tell, "selling their bodies for a fifth of rum. This ain't living, Mr. Harper."

This was a plea for help. If ever there was a one deserving of the secret, this child was. Mr. Harper didn't tell most folks what he knew, what Grandma Cora had taught him. They wouldn't believe. They might not even care. So he had waited.

"Regina, there's more to history than's in a book. Every day I come to this school, hoping that just one student might understand the purpose of the stories and the reason for the way I tell them." Regina smiled and the tears flowed freely now. "History's not about grades or getting a good job. History holds the key to the mystery of Flight. Can you guess what the purpose of the Flight is, Regina?" he asked, ever the teacher.

"To escape?"

"Escape from oppression, that's the way the old folks handed down the story. But this is a new day. A new millennium is looking us dead in the eye. Regina, we've been slaves too long and that's because our homesickness has made us go crazy. We've forgotten our manners and songs and stories and skills and language and civility and dignity. We long for Home with a yearning that wails, that cries the blues. But the Flight, Regina, that's the path to our healing."

At first, Regina looked confused, but as she thought, a question formed full in her mind.

"Mr. Harper, where would we fly to? The Motherland?"

"The way the old folks told the story, the slaves flew to Mother Africa. Today the Flight takes us to the place that our ancestors explored in their rituals and stories and songs and dances."

"Where, Mr. Harper? I gotta know!"

Mr. Harper didn't speak. Instead he put his books and papers into his briefcase. Leaving Regina standing there, face streaked with tears, he walked to the door.

"Meet me at the Japanese Gardens at Washington Park on Saturday at 6:00 A.M. sharp!" Regina bowed her head in relief. "No colored people's time, Regina, 6:00 A.M. sharp."

"Yes, sir," said Regina, barely able to contain her excitement.

That night, as Regina lay in her narrow bed, she thought about the Flight. She closed her eyes and tried to imagine how it would feel to fly through the night sky. How had they done it, those ancient Africans? Was it true? The story had to be true! But why had the instructions been omitted from the story? In the next room over, she heard her mother screaming at someone on the phone. The tiny apartment reeked with rum. Overhead, a bed was scraping rhythmically against the floor, punctuated with moans and groans. Music loud enough to shatter glass. Screeching sirens of police cars, fire trucks, and ambulances up and down the street. Regina imagined herself flying away to an island paradise she saw advertised on TV. Where *would* she go? Regina wondered.

Regina finally fell asleep, and as she slept, she dreamed that Mr. Harper appeared in her room. He was drenched in light and was wearing royal white and golden garb. He carried a staff in one hand and a dove in the other.

The room fell silent. The sounds of the streets faded to a distant whisper, then disappeared altogether. Such a sweet peace she had never known in this room. Mr. Harper said, "Regina, you are worthy to receive the secret of the Flight, but you must answer one question: Where will you fly to?"

"But, Mr. Harper, that's what I asked you!"

"You have to answer that question for yourself, and the answer is inside you. Right now you are dreaming. How do you feel?"

Regina thought a moment. "Actually, I feel pretty good."

"Okay, now *what* do you feel?"

"Love. Peace. Joy. Contentment. Awe. Excitement."

"Regina, if you could feel this way all the time, would you still want to escape?"

"Why, no, I don't think so. I mean, I don't want to stay in this neighborhood forever, but I could stay until I graduated from high school. Then I'll go away to college. I feel wonderful like this. I could hang tough if I could feel like this from time to time."

"This state is available to you at anytime. I'll teach you how to use the Flight to fly Home whenever you need to."

"Home? I am home," she said, confused.

"What is Home, Regina?"

"It's where you live."

"No, a house is where you live. What is Home?"

Regina thought and thought. Slowly and happily she smiled at Mr. Harper. "Home is where the heart is."

"Is your heart here in this bedroom, in this apartment, in this city?"

"No! I hate it here!" she said. "But I do feel happy in this dream. But I'm not in the real apartment, I'm in me. Hey! *I'm in me!*" Mr. Harper nodded.

"Home is where your heart feels the most peace and joy. That's within the highest and best part of you."

Suddenly, Regina experienced the strangest thing. Her heart was so full of love that her physical body could not contain it. She exploded into a million stars. She could see everywhere and knew everything. The universe was a kind and gentle place. No cursing, no rioting, no loneliness, no unwanted pregnancies, no crack cocaine, no fear. She felt *safe* here and realized she had never felt safe anywhere before.

And there were answers here. This place was like a gigantic library. All she had to do was ask a question and the answer would be given to her. More than anything she wanted to know how to help her mother. Her mother was a prostitute and an alcoholic, but deep down, there was so much love in the woman. Every once in a while she would completely surprise Regina with some little kindness. Her mother was worth saving. "Oh God," she prayed, "what can I do to help my mother?"

The answer was given to her immediately. First of all, her mother must want to change her life. God never undermines our free will, but we always have spiritual forces that are constantly nudging us to do better. Regina received the thought that her mother was on twenty-four-hour emergency alert; angels were ministering to her around the clock. And even though it might look like she was simply giving in to her worst urges, she really was fighting, and for that, her healing was guaranteed.

Regina's job was to reinforce the angels' work by sending her mother daily doses of love and light. This would help to create a healing atmosphere in their apartment. Even when her mother was at her worst, Regina had to see her as healed. Most important, Regina understood that although they were mother and daughter, connected by blood and love, they were two separate individuals with their own lives. She could love her mother, but ultimately, they were each responsible for their own lives.

Regina felt humbled and a deep gratitude. To say "thank you" wasn't enough, but she said it with all her heart. It felt as if an incredible burden had been lifted from her.

Blackness stretched to the edges of Regina's consciousness as sleep overtook her. "It's time to fly Home," said Mr. Harper. "It's time to fly Home." Her last thought was of Saturday and the work that lay ahead of her.

Credits

Step 1: Buying the Peas

"World Up!" by P. K. McCary, author, *Black Bible Chronicles: From Genesis to the Promised Land, Book One*. Published by African American Family Press. Reprinted by permission of P. K. McCary.

"When Souls Were Made," excerpt as submitted from *Mules and Men* by Zora Neale Hurston. Copyright ©1935 by Zora Neale Hurston. Copyright renewed 1963 by John C. Hurston and Joel Hurston. Reprinted by permission of HarperCollins Publishers, Inc.

"Session Nine," by Estella Conwill Majozo, *Jiva Telling Rites*, First Edition, First Printing. Copyright © 1991 by Estella Conwill Majozo. Reprinted by permission of Third World Press, Chicago.

"The Darkness of Space Produced Life," by the Honorable Elijah Muhammad, *The Theology of Time*. Copyright © 1992 by Abass Rassoull. Published and reprinted by permission of U.B. & U.S. Communications Systems, Inc., 912 West Pembroke Ave., Hampton, Virginia 23669, Telephone: (757) 723-2696.

"Birth Pains of the Civil Rights Movement" was reprinted by permission of The Putnam Publishing Group from *My Soul Is Rested* by Howell Raines. Copyright © 1977 by Howell Raines.

"How Sky and Earth Became One: A Yoruba Creation Story," by Ralph Cheo Thurmon. Copyright © 1996 by Ralph Cheo Thurmon. Reprinted by permission of the author.

Step 2: Sorting the Peas

"A Lesson in Consciousness," by Haki R. Madhubuti, from *Black Men: Obsolete, Single, Dangerous? The Afrikan American Family in Transition*, First Edition, Sixth Printing. Copyright © 1990 by Haki R. Madhubuti. Reprinted by permission of Third World Press, Chicago.

"How the 40oz Can Impair Good Judgement," by Alfred "Coach" Powell, from *Message 'n a Bottle: The 40oz Scandal*. Copyright © 1995 by Alfred "Coach" Powell. Reprinted by permission of Renaissance Press, Chicago.

"The 42 Principles of Ma'at," by Bandele Publications, "The 42 Principles of Ma'at chart," P.O. Box 21540, Washington, DC 20009, (301) 779-7530. Ma'at principles translated by Melanin Sisters Educational Consultants. Reprinted by permission of Bandele Publications.

"What You Think Is What You Get," by Janice C. Hodge. Copyright © 1996 by Janice C. Hodge. Reprinted by permission of the author.

"How to Search for Truth," reprinted from *George Washington Carver: In His Own Words* by Gary R. Kremer, by permission of the University of Missouri Press. Copyright © 1987 by the Curators of the University of Missouri.

"Lessons on the Playground of Life," by Michelle R. Dunlap. Copyright © 1996 by Michelle R. Dunlap. Reprinted by permission of the author.

Step 3: Soaking the Peas

"Crowning Glory," by Kecia Lynn. Copyright © 1996 by Kecia Lynn. Reprinted by permission of the author.

"A Place to Call My Own," by Beverly Phillips McLeod. Copyright © 1996 by Beverly Phillips McLeod. Reprinted by permission of the author.

"Breaking the Rules," from *Unbought and Unbossed*, by Shirley Chisholm. Copyright © 1970 by Shirley Chisholm. Published by Avon Books, A division of The Hearst Corporation. Reprinted by permission of the author.

"To Boldly Go," reprinted by permission of The Putnam Publishing Group from *Beyond Uhura* by Nichelle Nichols. Copyright © 1994 by Nichelle Nichols.

Step 4: Cooking the Peas

"From Welfare to Self Care," by Debora Tutterrow. Copyright © 1996 by Debora Tutterrow. Reprinted by permission of the author.

"Watchi (recipe)," reprinted with permission from Communicators Press and the Divine Jerusalem Sisterhood, *Soul Vegetarian Cookbook,* 1992.

"My Father, John Norton," by Ken Norton, excerpted from the forthcoming book *Norton.* Copyright © 1998 by Ken Norton. Reprinted by permission of the author and Marshall Terrill.

"Teaching Self-Worth Through Dance," by Ruth Beckford. Copyright © 1996 by Ruth Beckford. Reprinted by permission of the author.

"Sexual Beatitudes," from *Pushed Back to Strength* by Gloria Wade-Gayles. Copyright © 1993 by Gloria Wade-Gayles. Reprinted by permission of Beacon Press, Boston.

"New Directions," from *Wouldn't Take Nothin' for My Journey Now* by Maya Angelou. Copyright © 1993 by Maya Angelou. Reprinted by permission of Random House, Inc.

Step 5: Eating the Peas

"A Remedy for Racism," from *Nigger: An Autobiography* by Dick Gregory. Copyright © 1964 by Dick Gregory Enterprises, Inc. Used by permission of Dutton Signet, a division of Penguin Books USA Inc.

"Lessons in Joy from the Bionic Woman," by Ruth Beckford. Copyright © 1996 by Ruth Beckford. Reprinted by permission of the author.

"Finding the Proper Joy," reprinted with the permission of Scribner, a Division of Simon & Schuster from *Bertice: The World According to Me* by Bertice Berry. Copyright © 1996 by Bertice Berry Productions, Inc.

"A Well Earned Joy," from *Narrative of the Life of Frederick Douglass: An American Slave,* by Frederick Douglass. Dolphin Books edition: 1963. Originally published in 1845 by the Anti-Slavery Office: Boston. Public domain.

"Creating Joy," from *The Delany Sisters' Book of Everyday Wisdom,* by Sarah and Bessie Delany with Amy Hill Hearth. Published in 1994 by Kodansha America, Inc. Copyright © by Amy Hill Hearth, Sarah Louise Delany and Annie Elizabeth Delany.

"The Summer the Father Became a Mother," by Ralph Cheo Thurmon. Copyright © 1996 by Ralph Cheo Thurmon. Reprinted by permission of the author.

Step 6: Napping